OF ONE BLOOD ALL NATIONS

John Bingham:
Ohio Congressman's Diplomatic Career in Meiji Japan (1873-1885)

By Sam Kidder

Published by Piscataqua Press

An imprint of RiverRun Bookstore, Inc.

32 Daniel Street

Portsmouth, NH 03801

www.riverrunbookstore.com

www.piscataquapress.com

ISBN: 978-1-950381-58-6

Printed in the United States of America

To Miyako

TABLE OF CONTENTS

Introduction

John Bingham did more to shape America's initial diplomatic relationship with Japan than any other American. In Japan, the Meiji Restoration was transforming politics and society. In America, Reconstruction was bringing equally momentous political and social change. Bingham had been one of the most consequential political leaders in the immediate post-Civil War years. Appointed minister[1] to Japan by President Ulysses S. Grant, the Ohio congressman established the policy direction and built the institutional foundation of the two nations' bilateral ties.

In a *New York Times* guest editorial in 2013 Gerard Magliocca wrote, "More than anyone else except Abraham Lincoln, John Bingham was responsible for establishing what the Civil War meant for America's future."[2] Bingham's most important contribution came as primary author of the 14th amendment to the Constitution, establishing equal protection and due process as rights for all Americans. Bingham had been an advisor to President Lincoln, a trusted friend of Secretary of War Stanton, and the lone civilian prosecutor on the military tribunal that tried the Lincoln assassins. At the impeachment trial of President Andrew Johnson, he delivered the closing prosecution arguments to the Senate.

Before Bingham arrived in Japan in 1873, America's policy approach to the emerging island nation had been incoherent and haphazard. Under his leadership, it became consistent and ultimately successful. Bingham built America's first long-term physical diplomatic presence and nurtured the first generation of American diplomats with expertise in Japan affairs. By the time that he returned to his beloved Ohio in 1885, he had become America's longest serving chief diplomat in Japan, a distinction he still holds.

There is substantial literature on Bingham's role in crafting and passage of the 14th Amendment, his most studied and best recalled achievement. Richard Aynes, Dean Emeritus of Akron University School of Law, in various prestigious legal journals, and Gerard Magliocca, of Indiana University's Robert H. McKinney School of Law, in *American Founding Son* (2013), have written and analyzed Bingham — the constitutional legal mind. Yale's Akihl Reed Amar is just one of many others now recognizing Bingham's importance.

Unfortunately, John Bingham's contributions to the relationship between Japan and the United States have been largely neglected. Beyond Jack Hammersmith's excellent survey, *Spoilsmen in a "Flowery Fairyland,"*[3] there is little recent scholarship that focuses on Bingham's years in Japan. Ambassador Mike Mansfield whose service in Japan from 1977 to 1988 was months shorter than Bingham's term, was fond of saying that the relationship between Japan and the United States was the most important bilateral relationship in the world, "bar none." It was a mantra repeated by Japanese and American diplomats for generations. In order to better understand the crucial early years of that vital relationship it is important to examine the role of John Bingham. This book is an attempt to do that. I have no doubt that there are shortcomings in my coverage and analysis. But if I can provoke further interest and encourage additional study of John Bingham, America's envoy to Meiji Japan, then I can perhaps claim success for this effort.

CHAPTER ONE

Small Town Youth

John Armor Bingham arrived at Yokohama on September 27, 1873. The former Ohio congressman carried a letter from President Ulysses S. Grant to Japan's young Emperor Meiji. America's most prominent Civil War military hero, Grant was leading a prodigious political effort to reorder American society. Across the continent and beyond the broad Pacific Ocean, the ancient Empire of Japan was engaged in an equally momentous transformation. In 1868, the same year as Grant's election victory, the new emperor ascended the fabled Chrysanthemum Throne, becoming the symbolic embodiment and political epicenter of Japan's effort to remake its society. The Reconstruction Era in the United States and the Meiji Restoration in Japan were years of violence and social confusion. But they were also periods of great energy and expectation. Already a key player in America's post-Civil War events, Bingham was to become the architect of America's emerging diplomatic relationship with Japan. Who was this Ohio politician who arrived in Japan at such a seminal time?

Mercer, Pennsylvania - When John Armor Bingham was born at Mercer, Pennsylvania, on January 21, 1815, his parents felt relief and renewed hope. Hugh and Esther Bailey Bingham had been married for eight years before their first child was born. The wait was long and now they were pleased to have a healthy son. John's family, like many in the new towns in the western Pennsylvania hills, had strong Calvinist roots. Faith promised a future where God's purpose would prevail. Patriotism and pride in country and community was fresh. Education was respected. And hard work was demanded.

In western Pennsylvania, Mercer County had been newly formed as a separate jurisdiction in 1800.[1] Named for General Hugh Mercer, family friend of George Washington and Revolutionary War hero, many of Mercer's early residents came from similar roots as their county's namesake.[2] Directly across the street from the house where John was born,[3] the Mercer County Courthouse had been dedicated in 1807, the year Esther and Hugh Bingham were married. The county's name was a daily reminder of the still recent proud struggle against the British monarchy. The two-story brick courthouse dominated the small town and demonstrated the residents' civic commitment to strive to secure the blessings of liberty for generations of Mercer citizens to come.

Before John was born, his family had already been active in community affairs and politics. Thomas Bingham, Hugh's younger brother, became Mercer postmaster in 1810 and when the War of 1812 broke out, Hugh and Thomas Bingham hastened to Erie to support Commodore Oliver Perry's successful campaign against British naval control of the Great Lakes.[4] In 1811, Hugh Bingham began his association with Mercer Academy, the town's only school of note in those early days. He continued to serve as a trustee of the academy until 1819.[5] In 1822-23 the Pennsylvania legislature, spurred on by the imminent opening of the Erie Canal, authorized a survey to study a canal route to connect Lake Erie with the Ohio River. Hugh

Bingham was an enthusiastic booster of the project.[6]

The elder Bingham's political opinions were closely interwoven with his religious beliefs. A friend and one of Mercer's leading citizens was the Reverend Samuel Tait, pastor of the Bingham family's church. Tait was affiliated with the Presbyterian Church in the United States of America, with roots in the Church of Scotland. Tait also served as president of Mercer Academy.[7] At church Hugh Bingham joined Tait to form a missionary association under the leadership of the American Board of Commissioners of Foreign Missions (ABCFM). As for many other small towns like Mercer in the early decades of the nineteenth century, church's missionary activities provided a tantalizing window to a world beyond. Publications including *Missionary Herald* published by the ABCFM were among the limited reading materials available to the eager young John.[8] In 1820, Hugh Bingham is listed as Secretary of the newly formed Mercer, Pennsylvania, chapter of the American Bible Society, a national organization which boasted John Quincy Adams and Star Spangled Banner poet Francis Scott Key among its distinguished vice presidents.[9] The Society represented an interdenominational aspiration to reach out to other lands and cultures. The adults in John Bingham's world had an enthusiasm for politics, an appreciation of the role of national organizations, and a curiosity about the world beyond the fields that surrounded Mercer.[10]

As he turned ten years old, John Bingham's world had begun to expand. The Erie Canal, connecting New York City and the Hudson River Valley with the Great Lakes, opened in 1825. Mercer now seemed closer to the great cities of the eastern seaboard and the lands beyond the Atlantic Ocean, the lands of the English kings and Roman generals young John Bingham read about with such passion. Then on one magical night in June, the Marquis de Lafayette arrived in Mercer after midnight. Taking a brief rest at Hackett House before hurrying north to Erie, Lafayette was nearing the end of a triumphal tour of the new republic. As a young man, he had helped free America from British colonial rule and now an old man, he was an honored hero and an inspiration to the impressionable ten-year old boy.[11]

異国船打払令 (*Ikokusen Uchiharairei*)

In a distant corner of young John Bingham's world, Japan's centuries old policy of isolation was under increasing threat. Russian ships had appeared off Japan's northern coasts. The British had become more active along the China coast. The Tokugawa government, weak and increasingly desperate, in 1825, issued an order to expel all barbarian ships that approach the Japanese coast.[12]

Cadiz, Ohio - In 1827, John's mother died, and John was sent to live with his uncle Thomas Bingham and his growing family in Cadiz, Ohio. During his adolescent years with his uncle's family, the strains of politics and religion continued to influence Bingham. Cadiz was the seat of Harrison County, and was a one day's ride from two booming Ohio River towns, Stubenville, Ohio, and Wheeling, Virginia. Resettling in Ohio after leaving Mercer, Thomas Bingham had become a successful merchant. Like his older brother Hugh back in Pennsylvania, Thomas was involved in public service, serving as associate judge of the Harrison County Court of Appeals, from 1825 to 1839.[13] He was also a founding member of the Associate Reformed Presbyterian Church. [14]

In contrast to his more austere life in Mercer and the pain of the loss of his mother, for John the Cadiz Bingham household was a lively place. There were two sons not far from John's age, and three older daughters. In 1825, they welcomed a baby girl, Amanda, who was a toddler when John first came to live in Cadiz. Amanda was predestined to play a leading role in John Bingham's adult life. The sojourn in Cadiz left an indelible emotional imprint on young John Bingham.

Mercer, Pennsylvania – At age sixteen John Bingham took his first formal job and unsurprisingly, the work was political. Returning to Mercer in 1831 after his father's remarriage, young John took an apprenticeship with the *Luminary*, an anti-Masonic newspaper.[15] William Clark, a prominent Presbyterian layman, friend of Hugh Bingham, and editor of the *Luminary*, was a staunch opponent of slavery.[16] The *Luminary* also advocated government support for infrastructure development and vigorously opposed President Andrew Jackson, a slaveholder who flaunted his Masonic ties. In 1835, John Ritner, a veteran of the War of 1812 and a resident of southwestern Pennsylvania, was elected governor on the Anti-Masonic ticket. Ritner appointed Hugh Bingham to be Mercer County clerk of courts, evidence of the Bingham's political involvement. John Bingham was swept into a political environment that opposed slavery and promoted government support of infrastructure building, views that were to animate Bingham's political career.[17]

Anti-Masonry wasn't the only political game in Mercer. In February, 1835, Mercer men and women gathered as the Mercer Temperance Society to consider a resolution. The resolution stated that "the manufacture and sale of ardent spirits, except as medicine and for mechanical purposes, are a violation of the political economy, and impose an enormous burden upon the industry and wealth of the country."[18] William Clark's *Luminary*, had been a principal organizer of the Temperance Society.[19] As the meeting moved to a vote, one of the final speakers urging approval was John A. Bingham. This is the first record of his direct personal political involvement, a role that he would play to great effect in some of the most important legislative decisions of his generation.

New Athens, Ohio - College studies provided John Bingham with an intellectual framework for his political philosophy that remained with him throughout his political and diplomatic career. Enrolling in the small non-denominational but Presbyterian influenced Franklin College in New Athens, Ohio, in May of 1835, Bingham was heavily influenced by the Reverend John Walker. Walker, who earlier had served churches in Mercer and Cadiz, was charismatic, energetic, and aggressively anti-slavery. He maintained an Underground Railway "station" on his own property outside of town.[20] Studying history with Walker, Bingham was captivated by his professor's exposition of the sweep of human experience. Walker described a divine purpose working its way through the discipline of Roman Law and the stirrings of representative government in the Magna Carta. The unfinished sacred promise was to be the fulfillment of America's founding ideal, the equality of all men. At Franklin, Bingham was able to weld the intellectual principles of republicanism to the values he had absorbed from church and family in his years in Mercer and Cadiz.

The close relationships Bingham established and nourished during his two years at Franklin College provided him with a valuable social network and had a lasting impact on his personal and professional life. Although Franklin remained a tiny school, it produced three United States Senators, six Congressmen, a state governor and an organizer of the Republican Party among other graduates of note from various fields.[21] Additionally, almost fifty Franklinites from those years entered the ministry.

Bingham's friendship with Titus Basfield was particularly significant. About thirty years old in 1837 when he completed his courses at Franklin College, Basfield had been born a slave in Virginia. While still in bondage, he had been baptized by the Reverend David Carson, a minister in the Associate Presbyterian Church and a colleague of John Walker. After securing Basfield's freedom, Carson was offered a teaching position at Jefferson College and Basfield accompanied him to Pennsylvania. Soon after he entered Franklin College. During their shared time at Franklin, Bingham and Basfield developed a durable friendship. The two continued to correspond well into Bingham's years in Japan.[22] After two years in New Athens, John Bingham now had a concrete and direct personal understanding of the human dimension of slavery.

In June of 1835 the Mercer County Anti-Slavery Society adopted a resolution that included a passage from Acts Chapter 17 Verse 26 "God has made of one blood all nations of men". In 1840, a Constitution for the Kingdom of Hawaii was promulgated. Its opening line reads: "God hath made of one blood all nations of men to dwell on the earth, in unity and blessedness."[23] The words that had animated communities in Bingham's world in Ohio and Pennsylvania were crossing the Pacific.

Mercer, Pennsylvania - Returning to Mercer from Franklin College in 1838, young John Bingham was eager to find a political path forward. Reading law with John J. Pearson and William Stewart, Bingham passed the Pennsylvania bar in 1840. Pearson was fifteen

11

years Bingham's senior and had served a term in the House of Representatives from 1835-1836. Stewart was just five years older than Bingham and was also politically active and won a seat in the Pennsylvania State Senate beginning service there in 1841. These were Bingham's kind of people — anti-Masonic, anti-Jackson and anti-slavery.[24] But whatever benefit their legal and political guidance may have provided, they crowded Bingham's political path out of Mercer.

Cadiz, Ohio – Bingham turned to Cadiz where professional and political opportunities were more open. In 1840, the American economy was weak and many voters blamed Democratic incumbent President Martin Van Buren. In Cadiz, a young attorney, Edwin Stanton, was making a name for himself as an able supporter of the Democrats. For Stanton, this was a tentative first step up the political influence ladder whose top rung was to be service as Abraham Lincoln's secretary of war. Brash newcomer Bingham took to the speaking circuit in favor of Ohio and Whig presidential candidate William Henry Harrison, quickly earning a reputation as an engaging speaker. Grasping this chance "...in a large measure determined his subsequent career."[25] Just over ten years later, Stanton and Bingham's careers were to intersect again, the next time as allies not antagonists. The following description of Bingham's speaking style by a biographer who had spoken to many who had heard the Ohioan in person provides insight into Bingham's appeal.

> *His expression was clear and his language well chosen. His earnestness often amounted to intensity and his sarcasm was clean and cutting. His gestures were natural and graceful and to a handsome figure, always dressed in good taste, he*

*united a graceful manner. Though he was not a wit and did
not attempt to be, nevertheless his earnestness and telling
hits often provoked the wildest enthusiasm in his audience.
Politics to him was always serious business. He argued to
produce conviction and conversion. His aim was to build
up a party and assist in shaping its policy. His thoughts
reached out even to a future destiny of his country and the
welfare of its people. He wished to convert others to his way
of thinking; and in this he was noticeably successful.*[26]

In making his political calculation to move to Cadiz, Bingham also factored in personal considerations. His cousin's husband, Josiah Scott, an 1829 graduate of Franklin College, was practicing law in Cadiz. In 1834, Scott had been elected to serve as Harrison County prosecutor. In 1838, he was defeated for that office by the ambitious young Stanton. One biographer describes Scott as "indolent" so perhaps the family was looking to enlist Bingham to invigorate the practice.[27] Another biographer offers a more poetic possibility, "Like Ulysses, he imagined a siren call, that of Uncle Thomas's sparkling daughter, Amanda."[28] And his cousin Amanda whom he had known as a child during his stay with Thomas Bingham's family as a youth, became John's bride in 1844. In 1841, John Bingham passed the Ohio bar. He had now positioned himself to launch a career that would make him one of America's most significant national legislators.

New Philadelphia, Ohio - Between 1841 and 1851 John Bingham settled into professional and family life and established himself as an up and coming Ohio politician. President Harrison's untimely death just a month after his inauguration in March of 1841, and succession by John Tyler, a slaveholding Virginian, was undoubtedly discouraging. Still, remaining committed to the Whig party, in 1842 Bingham became the chair of the Harrison County party. In 1843, maintaining his relationship with Josiah Scott in Cadiz, Bingham joined a law office in New Philadelphia, seat of neighboring Tuscarawas County. By 1846, Bingham was able to win election as county prosecuting attorney. He now had established a political base in two Ohio counties, Harrison and Tuscarawas.[29]

During the New Philadelphia years, John Bingham made his first appearance on the national stage. It was a cameo role but one that set the tone for the rest of his career in elective office. The Whig Party was divided over the issue of slavery and had nominated Zachary Taylor, a war hero with indefinite political positions, as its presidential candidate. Bingham did not oppose the nomination but wanted the convention to adopt a clear platform opposing slavery. On June 9, 1848, the third day of the Whig convention in Philadelphia, he stood to introduce a resolution that called for "no extension of slave territory, no acquisition of foreign territory by conquest, protection to American industry" causing an uproar from the floor. Bingham was ruled out of order but the newspapers carried the text of his proposal and his name was now out to a broader, national public.[30] From his parents, teachers, and friends, Bingham had learned the values that would inspire his years of public service. In the next years, he honed his skills at the often-frustrating effort to mold these ideals into political reality.

Main Building of Franklin College, New Athens, Ohio. Author's photograph.

CHAPTER TWO

A Congressman of Consequence

Cadiz, Ohio - After the New Philadelphia interlude and a short career detour through Cincinnati, John Bingham stepped onto a political path that led directly to the corridors of power in Washington, D.C. In 1851, he and Amanda were back home in Cadiz and once more he took up work in the law office he shared with his wife's brother-in-law, Josiah Scott. Addressing the Jefferson and Philosophic Literary Societies at Franklin College the same year, he demonstrated that he had learned to "blend his anti-slavery ideals with practical politics."[1] In his Franklin College speech Bingham said that the "principle which informs the Constitution of ours and makes up its very vitality, is the political equality of the human race, a full recognition of the truth that God has made of one blood all nations of men."[2]

On his first step toward higher elected office, he stumbled but fell forward. Nominated by the Whigs as the party's candidate for the office of Judge of the Court of Common Pleas for the tri-county district of Harrison, Jefferson, and Tuscarawas Counties, he lost in the general election. Despite this loss, Bingham remained active in Whig politics. Attending the Whig state convention in Columbus in 1852, he was nominated as a presidential elector in support of Whig candidate and military hero Winfield Scott. But the Whigs remained split over the issue of slavery and Bingham was losing enthusiasm for the party.

When the Kansas-Nebraska Act became law in 1854 a new force for political realignment appeared. The Missouri Compromise of 1820 had stipulated that slavery was outlawed north of latitude 36 degrees 30 minutes. The Kansas-Nebraska Act stated that in the Kansas and Nebraska territories, both of which were north of that latitude, the citizens were to decide the legality of slavery within their own state's borders. The Act infuriated anti-slavery forces and led to a consolidation of several weaker political groups, including anti-slavery Whigs. In July, one thousand concerned Ohioans gathered in Columbus and formed an anti-Nebraska party.[3] In September John Bingham was selected as the party's nominee for the 21st Congressional District which consisted of Carroll, Columbiana, Harrison, and Jefferson Counties. In the fall election, Bingham soundly defeated Democratic incumbent, Andrew Stuart of Stubenville.[4] In one biographer's words, "The passing of the Kansas-Nebraska Act opened the door for John Bingham's rise to power."[5] By the summer of 1855 Bingham began his lifelong association with the newly formed Republican Party.

Washington, D.C. – When the 34th Congress convened its first session in March of 1855, John Bingham's family did not accompany him to Washington. The freshman Ohio congressman took rooms with Joshua Giddings, congressman from northeastern Ohio and a prominent anti-slavery voice. Giddings became an important mentor to the young Cadizian.

During the second session, in 1856, anti-slavery Massachusetts Senator Charles Sumner was attacked at his Senate desk by South Carolina Congressman Preston Brooks. Brooks had been angered by Sumner's comments in a Senate speech on the issue of slavery in Kansas. He felt Sumner's words had insulted his cousin, South Carolina Senator Andrew Butler. Brooks delivered multiple blows to Sumner's head with a hard, wooden cane. It was three years before Sumner was able to return to the Senate. The incident galvanized northern opinion against the slave states and Bingham's outspoken condemnation of Brooks, couched in constitutional terms, attracted attention. "For Bingham, Brooks was guilty not only of assault and battery, but also of an act of contempt against the Congress."[6]

John Bingham was reelected in 1856 but the Democrats took a majority in both the House and Senate. For Bingham that meant a demotion from assignment to the highly visible Committee on Elections he had held during in the 34th Congress. In the 35th Congress he was selected to serve on the Committee on Expenditures of the State Department. This committee assignment gave him practical insight into foreign policy formation.[7] Also, winning a seat in that election, from Mercer, Pennsylvania, was William Stewart, Bingham's mentor in Mercer when reading for the Pennsylvania bar.[8] In 1857, Bingham nominated a brash, young Ohioan, George Armstrong Custer, for admission to West Point. In keeping with Republican Party policies favoring protectionist measures in foreign trade, Bingham voted for tariff increases on coal, wool and iron, all products important to business interests in his congressional district.[9]

Reelected again in 1858, when the 36th Congress convened John Bingham brought Amanda with him to Washington for the first time, leaving the children at home with relatives. Foreshadowing the debate over citizenship rights where Bingham was to play such a critical role after the Civil War, the Ohio congressman opposed statehood for the Territory of Oregon. Oregon would not allow people of color to own property or file suit in Oregon courts. Bingham argued that the Oregon constitution violated the privileges and immunity clause of Article IV of the United States Constitution, in effect asserting that national citizenship prevented any state from taking away privileges granted to a citizen of any other state.[10]

In 1860, Bingham ran unopposed. Abraham Lincoln headed the ticket and the vice-presidential candidate, Hannibal Hamlin of Maine, had been a fellow boarder with Bingham at Washington House when the Ohio congressman was living away from his family while Congress was in session.[11] Bingham played an active role in overall Republican Party stumping well beyond his own district. Two of his well-known House speeches were reprinted as pamphlets for distribution nationally, available for 50 cents for 100 copies.[12]

In Washington, Bingham met often, sometimes privately, with incoming President Lincoln.[13] In putting together his cabinet, Lincoln sought Bingham's advice, particularly with his proposed choice of Salmon Chase to be secretary of the treasury. Appointing Chase to Treasury would open an Ohio senate seat and Bingham would be among the possible successor candidates. Bingham's endorsement of Chase for Treasury was unrequited as Chase's Ohio Senate seat was passed to John Sherman, brother of William T. Sherman who was soon to become one of America's most recognized military leaders.

With the Civil War underway for less than a year, Lincoln decided to replace Secretary of War Simon Cameron. He called Bingham to the White House to consult on the advisability of Edwin Stanton as the replacement. Knowing Stanton well and favorably, the Ohio congressman gave Stanton a strong endorsement. In the House, Bingham proved a valued ally including acting as house manager for the high-profile impeachment of Tennessee United States District

Judge West H. Humphreys and providing strong support on Capitol Hill, as a member of the Joint Senate and House Committee for Lincoln's suspension of *Habeus Corpus*.[14]

By the autumn of 1862, the poor progress of the northern war effort threatened to hurt the Republicans at the ballot box. Ohio had no provisions for absentee voting for soldiers serving away from Ohio. Bingham's district had been redrawn and his opponents were arguing that the incumbent congressman's stance on immediate and unconditional emancipation was too radical. Defeated for re-election Bingham remained active in the lame duck session, managing the successful House floor process for approving statehood for West Virginia.[15] In January 1864, Lincoln appointed Bingham judge advocate of the Military Department of the Susquehana at the rank of major. Stanton likely was behind the judge advocate appointment since the Army was about to begin the politically sensitive court martial of Surgeon General William Hammond and Stanton knew and trusted Bingham. Hammond was a key supporter of General George McClellan who was planning to run against Lincoln in the next election.[16]

In 1864, Bingham was once again elected to the House of Representatives. Ohio had changed its voting regulations allowing soldiers in the field to vote. But 1864 had also seen tragedy with the deaths in March from typhoid of the Bingham's seven-year-old daughter, Jessie, and six-year-old son, Preston. And even as Union victory was becoming more and more assured, the national tragedy was not over. On the evening of April 14, 1865, President Lincoln was shot. He died the next morning. That same day, at home in Cadiz, John Bingham received a telegram from Secretary of War Stanton telling him to come to Washington immediately.[17]

As war was raged in the United States, in Japan, Emperor Komei issued an edict to Revere the Emperor and Expel the Barbarians, Sonnō jōi (尊皇攘夷). The order over a generation earlier to repel all foreign ships had failed. Japan was experiencing social and political convulsions as momentous for her history as the Civil War and Reconstruction were for America

Bingham played a prominent role in the trial of the Lincoln assassins, the opening act of the post-Civil War political drama. Secretary of War Stanton wanted Bingham involved. As the lone civilian member of the prosecutorial team, Bingham joined a nine-member military tribunal. Chaired by Major General David Hunter and including Major General Lew Wallace, later famous as the author of the novel, *Ben Hur*, on the panel also was Brigadier General Albion Howe, who was involved in the politically explosive court martial trial of Surgeon General Hammond, a trial where John Bingham had served as prosecutor.[18] Judge Advocate General Joseph Holt led the prosecution assisted by military lawyer Henry Burnett and Bingham.[19]

For Bingham, the answer to the controversial question of the legitimacy of a military rather than civilian jurisdiction in the trial was clear. He had helped draft the *Habeus Corpus* Act of 1863 and asserted that despite the surrender of arms, the rebellion was not over until elected branches of government had deemed it to be so.[20] Bingham proved "...the most combative of the three prosecutors..."[21] and gave the prosecution's final argument. Four of the conspirators were hanged on July 7, 1865, less than three months after Lincoln's assassination. The controversies over the legitimacy of a military rather than a civilian tribunal and the execution by the federal government for the first time of a female, Mary Surratt, continued to provoke debate. But Bingham had acted within character and consistent with his stated beliefs.

Prosecutors for trial of the Lincoln assassins. L-R, John Bingham, Judge Joseph Holt, Brigadier General Henry Burnett. Library of Congress photograph.

John Bingham's greatest contribution to his country was his authorship of the first portion of the 14th Amendment. In 2015, Yale historian David Blight wrote that "No more important language exists to this day in the Constitution than Bingham's two sentences."[22] Ratified in 1868, "The 14th Amendment slumbered in the Constitution for more than half a century without beginning to bear out the hopes of its framers."[23] Associate Justice William Brennan who served on the Supreme Court from 1957-1990 held "that more cases have been litigated under the 14th Amendment than under any other provision of the United States Constitution."[24] Supreme Court Associate Justice Hugo Black (1937-1971) helped arouse the 14th Amendment from its slumber and in modern times to recognize the importance of Bingham's role, dubbing the Ohio congressman the second Madison.[25]

Today constitutional scholars recognize that this amendment is "arguably the most important amendment in the nation's history. It enshrined the notion of equality under the law, protected the rights of the newly freed slaves and guaranteed due process to all people."[26] Creation of a more equal society in America continues to be elusive. And it is imperative that we acknowledge the efforts and sacrifices of thousands of women and men over many decades to realize the ideals of equal protection and due process for all. Still, John Bingham's contribution deserves recognition.

All persons born or naturalized in the United States, and subject to the jurisdiction thereof, are citizens of the United States and of the states wherein they reside. No state shall make or enforce any law which shall abridge the privileges or immunities of citizens of the United States; nor without due process of law; nor deny to any person within its jurisdiction the equal protection of the laws.

- From Section 1 of the 14th Amendment to the United States Constitution

Months before the final ratification of the 14th Amendment, John Bingham had played a leading role in the impeachment trial of President Andrew Johnson. Calls for Johnson's impeachment had risen during the 39th Congress but Bingham had not joined the chorus. With the seating of the 40th Congress in March, 1867, Radical Republican voices, swelled by an even larger veto-proof margin in the House of Representatives, became louder. By early 1868, Bingham believed impeachment was necessary. After the House vote to impeach, John Bingham and anti-slavery firebrand, Pennsylvania Representative Thaddeus Stevens, formally conveyed the House's action to the Senate.

In accordance with the Constitution, it then fell to the Senate to conduct the trial. Presiding was Supreme Court Chief Justice Salmon

P. Chase, Bingham's earlier political associate in Ohio Republican politics. Counsel for the defense was William Evarts who less than ten years later would be appointed as secretary of state by President Hayes and become John Bingham's principal from 1877-1881. The Senate failed by a single vote to convict and Johnson remained in office. But once again, during the impeachment process, Bingham had demonstrated that he was one of the most important political figures of his generation. Next, Washington moved on to the election of 1868.

John Bingham won re-election in 1868 but by the smallest margin of his career.[27] When the 41st Congress convened he became chairman of the powerful House Judiciary Committee. In 1869, his eldest daughter Lucinda married the Reverend Samuel Robinson Frazier, a Franklin College graduate, who took up a pastorate with a Presbyterian church in Pittsburgh. In October 1870, Bingham was again re-elected, this time with a somewhat more comfortable margin. In 1871, accompanied by wife Amanda he made a political tour of the West, stumping for the Republican ticket in California. And as usual there were always the seemingly endless constituent demands, unsuccessfully championing a tariff on wool to protect his district's sheep raising industry from foreign competition and intervening with the Army to get a compassionate discharge for a constituent's consumptive son.[28] But back home there were those who felt Bingham had served long enough and that the seat in Congress should pass to a man from another county in the 16th District.

Then in the election of 1872 John Bingham lost the Republican Party nomination to Captain Lorenzo Danford of Belmont County.[29] His remarkable career in Congress showed he was committed firmly to ideals of equality but was practical in pursuing his goals. He was a steadying political presence during a tumultuous time. Lincoln turned to him for advice and Stanton called on him when he needed a reliable person to do a difficult job. Bingham was ambitious but not given to self-aggrandizement. His speeches were long but his humor often self-effacing. Perhaps his congressional career would be more storied if he had staked out an uncompromising position or championed a controversial but doomed issue. But Bingham believed that the law, and particularly the law as enshrined in the Constitution, must be paramount. For the congressman from Cadiz, compromise did not mean defeat.

CHAPTER THREE

Japan Comes to Washington

Washington, D.C. – John Bingham lost his Congressional seat in the 1872 election but did not abandon his ambition. Still physically vigorous, despite his deep emotional connection to Cadiz, a return to a small-town legal practice was not inviting. He knew that he had made a difference. He now searched for a way to continue to do so.

The first months of 1873 found Bingham back in Washington for the lame duck session of Congress. It was an opportunity to explore possible government appointments. He had not inherited a fortune and although his lifestyle was modest so also were his income and assets. Initially, there was talk about a judicial appointment. During the Civil War and in the Lincoln assassins' trial, Bingham had earned a reputation that led many to call him Judge Bingham. But as talk of a judgeship faded, the prospect of a diplomatic posting emerged. Now he might be able to add foreign affairs credentials to his résumé. This would perhaps be useful if he were to run again for elective office. For qualifications, he had knowledge and experience. More importantly, he had friends.

As John Bingham began to focus on a diplomatic posting, the important question became where. In his diary, Grant administration Secretary of State Hamilton Fish wrote about a conversation he had with President Grant during a cabinet meeting. Bingham's name had been raised as a possible appointment as minister to Russia. The Ohioan was deemed ineligible since he had been in the House at the time of a vote to raise the salary of that position.[1] In his memoirs, written later after a long diplomatic career, John Watson Foster wrote that Bingham had approached Indiana Senator Oliver P. Morton to ask that he sound out Foster on a possible appointment switch. By that time, Bingham had been tapped for Japan and Foster for Mexico. Foster wrote that Bingham was suggesting the switch since "... being an old man, feared that Japan being so far away ... he would be forgotten by his friends and constituents at home."[2] Foster rejected Bingham's appeal.

Bingham did not push to be appointed to the Japan position, but he also did not hold out for a different assignment. Although his knowledge was spotty, he knew Japan at least as well, and perhaps better, than most of his political colleagues and recognized the potential benefits of serving there. His involvement with the anti-Asian racial issue when he voted against admission of the Oregon Territory and the campaign trip he made to California shortly after the opening of the transcontinental railroad gave him some familiarity with issues across the Pacific.

Since childhood, Bingham had been an avid reader and he had followed American diplomacy as American leaders were beginning to pay attention to the Pacific region. By the 1840s, American whalers out of Boston and New York, sailing around Cape Horn, had become dominant in the Pacific, constituting as much as seventy-five percent of all whale hunting vessels. To American readers, Japan was "that doubled bolted land" in Herman Melville's novel, *Moby Dick*.[3] Hawaii had emerged as an important stopping off point. And John Bingham was certainly familiar with the controversial first missionary in the Hawaiian Islands from 1820-1840. His name was Hiram Bingham, not a relative but a name in the news.[4]

Daniel Webster, who served as secretary of state from 1841 and again from 1850-1852, had been a pioneer in articulating an American policy toward East Asia and the Pacific.[5] Young John Bingham had been an avid reader of Webster's speeches. In 1841 Hong Kong was ceded to the British and by 1843 Shanghai was opened to foreign commercial activity. In 1846 America's northern boundary dispute with Great Britain was settled. The United States took control of territory south of the 49th parallel providing access to Puget Sound and the mouth of the Columbia River. Then in 1848 under the terms of the Treaty of Guadalupe Hidalgo, Mexico ceded California and much of the land we now refer to as the American Southwest to the United States. Gold was discovered at Sutter's Mill. The rush was on and by 1850 California became a state. Representative Bingham no doubt shared the expansionist sentiments New York Senator and later Secretary of State William H. Seward expressed in his speech to the upper house on California statehood admission.

The Atlantic States, through their commercial, social and political affinities and sympathies are steadily renovating the Governments and the social constitutions of Europe and Africa. The Pacific States must necessarily perform the same sublime and beneficent functions in Asia. If, then, the American people shall remain an undivided nation, the ripening civilization of the West, after a separation growing wider and wider for four thousand years, will, in its circuit of the world, meet again and mingle with

the declining civilization of the East on our own free
soil, and a new and more perfect civilization will arise to
bless the earth, under the sway of our own cherished and
beneficent democratic institutions.[6]

With Commodore Mathew C. Perry's visits in 1853 and 1854 and Townsend Harris' dogged and ultimately successful effort to sign the Treaty of Amity and Commerce between Japan and the United States in 1858, Japan and America began a formal relationship. Mathew C. Perry was a younger brother of Oliver Hazard Perry, the hero of the Battle of Lake Erie in 1812, a battle seared into the lore of John Bingham's Mercer, Pennsylvania, childhood. Then in 1860, a mission of Japanese arrived in Washington for the formal signing of the treaty. Staying at the Willard Hotel, the Japanese delegation leaders met with President Buchanan in the Oval Office. The visiting Japanese made quite a stir in local society, traveling on to Baltimore, Philadelphia and then to New York before making the long trip back across Panama to San Francisco and on to Japan.[7]

Although American interest in Japan faded as the country became preoccupied with the daily crises of the Civil War, two developments during those dark years were important to Bingham's later engagement with the island nation. Japan's Tokugawa government, in power for two and a half centuries, was facing the unprecedented western naval domination of the high seas. In 1863, a battle took place between foreign ships from four western countries and shore batteries of the powerful *Choshu*[8] domain. Based in the western part of Japan's main island, Honshu, Choshu was one of the local powers whose independence threatened control by the central Tokugawa authorities.

The altercation at the Straits of Shimonoseki resulted in a political impasse that continued to fester for two decades. The British, French, Dutch and Americans extracted a sizeable indemnity from the Japanese for damages incurred in the fighting. With Tokugawa's military-led government already on its deathbed, the Shimonoseki Indemnity payments were an added burden for Japan's stumbling rulers. America's role in the fighting had been comparatively minor and the payments became an issue of contention in American politics. America's missionary groups, which had considerable influence on the State Department, were able to keep the issue alive in Washington. Many religious and educational leaders argued that the indemnity was unfair and wondered even if the Japanese should be forced to continue to pay, should the proceeds be used to modernize Japan's educational system. The groups that advocated this position were important allies of Bingham.

With the Civil War over and the political struggle to win the peace in full swing, Secretary of State William Seward once again turned America's attention to the Pacific. During the Civil War, Seward had concentrated on denying European diplomatic support for the Confederacy. Alaska was Seward's first target. America's purchase of Alaska from Russia was controversial and termed Seward's Folly. The incorporation of Alaska as a territory was, however, a fundamental component of Seward's aspirations for America in the Pacific. The inauguration of regular steamer service across the great circle route to Asia by the Pacific Mail and Steam-Ship Company in 1867 and the opening of the transcontinental railroad in 1869 further awakened America to a new role in Asia. In the fall of 1870, now a former secretary of state, Seward set out on a fourteen-month tour of the globe. He began the tour with a Pacific crossing and a first stop in Japan. By 1872, the *Tribune*, a New York based newspaper, posted young reporter, Edward H. House, to Japan.[9] American readers were now updated on developments in a country that was becoming more and more intriguing.[10]

John Bingham was still in Congress when the Iwakura Mission visited the United States in 1872. Led by Count *Iwakura Tomomi[11]*, one of Japan's leading figures of the Meiji Restoration period, the Japanese hoped that this mission to the United States and Europe would lead to the end of the unequal treaties. Following the first of the unequal treaties which had been negotiated by the American Harris, treaties between Japan and other foreign powers were concluded in rapid succession. The treaties established enclaves where foreign residents were exempt from Japanese legal jurisdiction and reserved to foreign governments the right to set tariffs. To the Japanese the treaties were humiliating and a major factor in the fall of Tokugawa rule.

Although the Iwakura Mission failed to achieve its primary purpose of getting agreement to revise the unequal treaties, it was a seminal chapter in Japan's relationship to the rest of the world. In America, the mission introduced America's political class to Japan. After an initial courtesy call by Iwakura on President Grant on March 4, 1872, and then eleven subsequent sessions with Secretary of State Hamilton Fish which continued until late July, Washington was awash with interest in Japan.[12] Upon arrival in Washington in late February, John Bingham was included on the guest list for the mission's reception hosted by the Japanese legation at the Masonic Hall on March 5.[13] And on March 6, the House of Representatives returned the courtesy, hosting a reception for the Japanese mission. From the missionary group, Bingham had been hearing about the Shimonoseki Indemnity for years in Congress. Now he had heard these concerns directly from Japanese.

During 1871-1872 David Thompson led a delegation of Japanese students and bureaucratic officials to the United States and Europe. Thompson's mission was one of several forerunners to the epochal Iwakura Mission in 1872-1873 headed by Meiji leaders. In a photograph taken in Berlin, Thompson is pictured with officials with surnames and local districts in Japanese on the reverse. Back row, left to right: Kagawa, Okayama; Thompson; Niwa, Nagoya. Front row, Ban, Kochi; Hoshiai, Tokushima; Tsuda, Okayama. Presbyterian Historical Society photograph.[1]

While certainly aware of America's increasing geopolitical involvement in the Pacific and with Japan, Bingham also had more personal connections. David Thompson, a young man from Bingham's hometown of Cadiz, arrived in Japan as a Presbyterian missionary in 1863. Thompson's family was active in the church in Cadiz where John's uncle Thomas Bingham had been among the founders. Like Bingham, Thompson had also attended Franklin College, graduating in 1859. [14] Thompson's relationship with Bingham was to become vital in the years ahead. But in the dark Civil War years, the reports from Thompson to friends and family in Cadiz gave John Bingham an appreciation of Japan and its potential far beyond that of all but a few of his political peers.

Another young man whose family was closely associated with Bingham was L.L. Janes who came to Kumamoto on Japan's southern island of Kyushu as an instructor in 1871. Janes' father was an ardent abolitionist and had been friends with Bingham since his days in New Philadelphia from 1845-1850.[15] Just as Bingham was leaving for his first term in Congress, young Janes joined Bingham's law office in Cadiz to begin reading law. As Bingham considered the offer of assignment to Japan, this personal connection undoubtedly made Japan feel a bit less distant.[16]

Bingham also was responsible for launching the diplomatic career of another young man born in Cadiz. Eli T. Sheppard had married the daughter of Bingham's law partner, Lewis Lawton. Bingham recommended Sheppard to President Grant for an appointment to the diplomatic service and in 1869, Sheppard was posted to China. Sheppard's advice became useful to Bingham when the defeated Congressman came under consideration for a diplomatic assignment.[17]

As Bingham was conducting his job search, Eli T. Sheppard, by then Consul in *Tientsin (Tianjin),* China, encouraged Bingham to seek the Chief of Mission position in China. In a November 15, 1872, letter to Bingham, Sheppard extolled the appeal of life and work in China. Sheppard believed the China slot would open soon with the anticipated resignation of Minister Frederick F. Low, former governor of California. Well aware that Bingham was not wealthy, Sheppard informed Bingham that the cost of living in Peking (Beijing) was manageable and that his family would find the housing comfortable.[18] Further, in a subsequent letter dated December 2, Sheppard assured his senior that the Chinese would welcome him. According to Sheppard, Bingham was already known to Chinese readers. Sheppard had commissioned a Chinese translation of a speech the Ohioan had delivered in Elyria, Ohio, in July of 1872, in support of Grant's re-election. The Tientsin consul wrote of Bingham's speech that "It is the first English spoken oration that was ever printed in the Language of Confucius."[19] Ten weeks later Sheppard reported to Bingham that he had heard from Minister Low that the lame duck Ohio Congressman had been selected to go to Rome so "I suppose my happy dream of having you in China as my minister, is over!"[20]

Not Russia, not Mexico, not China, not Rome, John Bingham was named and confirmed as minister to Japan. Japan remained peripheral to America's larger foreign policy interests but by 1873 was no longer obscure. The Iwakura Mission had made sure of that. And the appointment of such a distinguished figure as John Bingham raised the profile and the prestige of America's fledgling relationship with Japan and the Pacific.

CHAPTER FOUR
Off to Japan

Cadiz, Ohio - Three principal tasks remained for Bingham to complete before boarding the train for San Francisco to catch the steamer for Japan. First, he had to take leave of friends and family. In June, Franklin College awarded him a Doctor of Law degree and the citizens of Cadiz held a large party for the departing Bingham family. David Thompson, who was visiting Ohio at the time, wrote to his fellow Franklin graduate to congratulate the minister-designate and told him that by serving in Japan, he would be in a position to do God's work.[1] The departing family said goodbye to John and Amanda's eldest daughter, Lucinda (Lucy) and her husband, Samuel R. Frazier. Sisters Emma and Marie, both single and in their twenties, packed up for the adventure.

Physical preparation to leave Cadiz was the second principal task. Bingham rented out his house, another indication of his financial status; the Ohio politician was not among diplomats who could afford to leave their considerable estates in the hands of a caretaker and staff. For the new minister, his packing attention focused on his books. A list of the books he took with him provides a telling glance into his intellectual interests. His formal education had been more haphazard than many of his Washington, D.C. colleagues, particularly those from larger cities in the East. But he had great enthusiasm for reading, particularly literature and history. Volumes he shipped included works by the founding fathers Madison and Jefferson; the writings of Webster and Clay; books on Roman law and Greek art, European and world history; works by famous poets and books on Christianity. He also sent along works by British social philosophers Francis Bacon and Edmund Burke. And for lighter reading he brought Washington Irving.[2]

Third, Bingham had staff positions to fill. He would need a personal secretary and thought that Cadiz resident William Lucas would be the right fit for the job. Lucas, of mixed-race parents, was born free in Virginia in 1850 but was not able to attend school there. Moving to Cadiz, he went to work for the Bingham family and John Bingham made sure that Lucas was able to attend school. Lucas became the first non-white graduate of Cadiz's high school. While her son was visiting relatives in Virginia, Bingham approached William's mother to ask her to contact him so that he could offer a position to her son. Lucas later recalled, "My mother, in her ignorance, supposed of Japan, of which she had never heard, was somewhere clear outside this world… refused to give him the proper address."[3] Lucas went on to become an established leader in his small-town Ohio community.

Bingham had better luck finding a deputy to serve as legation secretary. Durham White Stevens had grown up in Washington, D.C., and then attended Oberlin College in Ohio, graduating in 1871. His father, E. L. Stevens, had also attended Oberlin and in 1834 signed a petition at Oberlin demanding emancipation of slaves. E. L. Stevens is also recorded the following year as a charter member of the Oberlin Anti-Slavery Society.[4] Bingham had known the elder Stevens at least from his years in Washington. In 1856 he wrote Bingham, addressing him as "Friend Bingham" and referring to their common companion, "father Giddings." who had been freshman Congressman Bingham's house mate during his first term in Congress.[5] Returning to Washington, D. W. Stevens studied law at Columbian University (renamed George Washington University in 1904) and was admitted to the Washington bar in 1873. Impressed by Stevens' legal background and interest in foreign languages, Bingham tried to approach Stevens at Oberlin but was initially only able to reach his father. His father managed to get in touch with his son and inform him of the offer of appointment, which President Grant approved. The young lawyer caught up with the Bingham family party before they left San Francisco aboard the steamship *Japan* on September 1.[6] Stevens was embarking on a remarkable career. His involvement with Japan would end tragically but not for many years.

Crossing the Pacific Ocean - The passage from San Francisco to Yokohama took four weeks, providing one last informal classroom for Bingham to prepare for his years in Japan. In addition to his chosen aide Stevens, Bingham and his family were joined on the voyage by Mrs. Helen "Nellie" Denison, the young wife of Henry Denison. Denison was already stationed in Yokohama as a legal advisor to the American Consulate in that port city just south of Tokyo. Denison had studied law in Washington, D.C., and worked for the Treasury Department before going to Japan. The newly wedded Denison had also played professional baseball for the Washington Olympians. He was hoping to move into the deputy slot at the Yokohama Consulate in the coming months.

The most important relationship Bingham was able to cultivate crossing the Pacific Ocean was with Thomas Walsh, prominent businessman. Walsh, who had been living in Japan, was returning from the States where he was attending to his business interests. He had also been in Washington where he lobbied for an increase in funding for the United States mission in Japan. In its July 7, 1873, edition, the *Japan Mail* reported that Walsh had written to President Grant asking that $20,000 be allocated to upgrade the U.S. Legation's premises.[7] Walsh had been doing business in Japan since 1862 and knew both the foreign and Japanese business communities well. He had hosted a lavish event for the Seward party at his "very large house" in Yokohama in 1870 as the former secretary of state and his party prepared to continue their world tour, departing for China via Kobe.[8] Walsh provided the incoming minister with both commercial analysis and gossipy details.

Yokohama, Japan - When John Bingham and his family stepped off the docks at Yokohama on September 27, they were on solid ground at long last. However, in the eyes of international law at the time, they were not yet fully on Japanese soil. The unequal treaties, signed between the Japanese government before the Meiji Restoration, restricted foreign residence to designated areas. Within these treaty ports, foreigners were not subject to Japanese legal jurisdiction. Since the institution of the treaties in the 1850s, Yokohama had grown to be the most vibrant of these communities. At the time of Bingham's arrival, Yokohama had approximately three thousand European and North American residents, an estimated ten percent of whom were American. The Chinese population was comparable in number to the westerners.[9] There were western style shops, trading houses, and regular steamer service to America, the China coast, and other Japanese ports. The overwhelming majority of the 250 to 300 western firms in Yokohama were British. Many of these were branches with head operations in Shanghai and Hong Kong and tentacles embracing the British Empire. The British dominated the boisterous English language local print media as well.

Yokohama port life was rambunctious. At least one thousand seamen passed through Yokohama in an average month. Chronicling his visit to Yokohama a decade earlier, Anglican Bishop of Victoria (Hong Kong), William Smith, wrote that Japanese officials "have endeavored to render Yokohama an attractive locality to young unmarried foreigners by establishing at the edge of the settlement and on a site approached by a narrow drawbridge over the canal, one of those infamous public institutions…containing its two hundred female inmates dispersed over a spacious series of apartments and all under government regulation and control."[10] By 1873 some of the missionaries and wealthy merchants had taken up residence on the Bluff overlooking Yokohama harbor. This group included Dr. James Hepburn, Presbyterian missionary and medical doctor who was busily preparing a Japanese-English dictionary and with others was translating the Bible into Japanese. The romanization Hepburn developed for his dictionary is still in use today. With exceptions such as the Walsh family, relations between the missionaries and the merchants were often strained and the two groups "regarded each other with cold hostility; at worst, open disgust."[11] As the senior American official, both groups, as well as the itinerant sailors and occasional tourists and official visitors, were to become John Bingham's new constituents. And under the unequal treaty system, they were also under his legal and judicial authority.

Tokyo - Still called Edo by many, Tokyo, literally "eastern capital", was home to a smaller but growing foreign population than Yokohama.

Several years before Bingham's arrival, a small foreign community had taken root in *Tsukiji* along Tokyo Bay near the newly opened *Shimbashi* railway station. The Meiji government had thought it would be useful to provide a separate residential area for foreigners now that many were becoming employed by the government. Although outside of treaty port jurisdiction, the relative isolation of the Tsukiji settlement offered Japanese authorities some degree of control. To encourage foreigners to stay close to home, the government, as had been done in Yokohama, originally set up pleasure quarters nearby. The area boasted brothels and teahouses where as many as two hundred *geisha*, twenty-one of them male, were employed. By the time Bingham arrived in Japan, the missionary group had taken root in Tsukiji and the entertainment quarter abandoned.[12]

While close to the seat of government, Tsukiji was also conveniently located to interact with the treaty port area south of the capital. Shimbashi Station, close by the foreign quarter, was the northern terminus of the first railway in Japan. The route connected Tokyo and Yokohama and was opened in October 1872, less than a year before Bingham arrived. Several years earlier, a Presbyterian missionary, Christopher Carrothers and his wife, Julia, had become the first missionaries to settle in this newly opened foreign-settlement area. A small missionary contingent soon began to move into Tsukiji. Guido Verbeck, a missionary of the Dutch Reformed Church[13] and an influential educator had encouraged the Japanese to launch the Iwakura Mission.[14] He had worked with David Thompson, Bingham's fellow Cadizian, and others, in recently organizing the Tokyo Union Church in Tsukiji. And the Presbyterians had determined that Tsukiji would be the center of their missionary efforts in Japan.[15]

In addition to the missionary contingent, an additional important category of foreigners settling in Tsukiji were so-called *oyatoi gaikokujin* or foreign experts hired by the Japanese government as advisors or technicians. Although scattered around the country, the *oyatoi* did coagulate around the central government in Tokyo to be close to their workplaces. Some of these advisors lived in quarters provided by the government agencies where they were employed. But some also settled in Tsukiji. In 1874, the Meiji government employed just over 500 of these foreign experts, fewer than ten percent of whom were Americans. More than half of the *oyatoi* were from the United Kingdom. The second largest group, the French, had largely cornered the Meiji market for military advisors.[16] Americans did dominate the Hokkaido Development Commission or *Kaitakushi*. Chartered by the Meiji government to develop Japan's northern most main island of Hokkaido, many foreigners working at this agency lived in *Shiba*, south of Tokyo's central district in the early years of the planning of the project. They did so to escape the harsh northern climate in the winter.

Beyond Yokohama and Tokyo, there were contingents of foreigners at various locations around the country. Terms of the treaty with America allowed additional operation of American consulates in Hakodate in Hokkaido, at Kobe (Hyogo) and Nagasaki on Kyushu. The Hakodate consulate operated more or less as a frontier outpost, but both Kobe and Nagasaki boasted lively foreign communities. The minister at the Legation in Tokyo had overall management authority over the consulates but the Legation's ability to control consulate operations was often limited. Appointments to the posts of consul, or consul general in the case of Yokohama, were under the control of the State Department back in Washington. The minister often had difficulty asserting practical supervision over these officers who could and did communicate directly with the Department without the approval or sometimes even the knowledge of the minister. Slowness of communications was an additional factor. Nagasaki was equidistant to Tokyo and Shanghai and its foreign community smaller but independent and well established. Yokohama had the money and the people and played New York's role to Tokyo's Washington in those same years. From time to time there were directives from Washington to all posts or requests for responses where the Legation in Tokyo was asked to coordinate a national reply. But day in and day out the consulates had considerable autonomy which was to present the minister with a management challenge in the years to come.

CHAPTER FIVE

An Unanticipated Crisis

Yokohama – Before he could exercise any authority, the newly arrived Minister remained in diplomatic protocol limbo. First, he had to present his credentials in an audience with the Emperor. Charles DeLong, Bingham's predecessor as minister, had been informed of his removal only when the news arrived with the Binghams. A native of New York State and an associate of Secretary of State Fish, DeLong had escorted the Iwakura Mission when that group was in the United States. He had returned to Japan when the mission sailed on to Europe in August of 1872. After Bingham's arrival, it was several months before DeLong was able to complete arrangements to return to the United States.[1] In the meantime, at a ceremony on October 7, 1873, the former Ohio congressman presented the letter he carried from President Grant to the Emperor. With Emperor Meiji's acceptance of these credentials, John Bingham was by international law and custom, America's minister to the Empire of Japan.

Even before arriving in Japan, John Bingham had been eager to make progress on policy issues. For him diplomacy at its root was a moral crusade. His letter to Franklin College classmate and friend, Thomas Campbell, makes clear how the Ohioan saw his duty in Japan.

My mission to the Imperial Court of Japan will be based on the triad – God, America, Japan. The Deity demands that the principles of justice, honesty, and candidness must be invoked. God's agent, America, must be allowed to deal with Japan so as to reverberate to the greatest glory of the United States and Japan. America must break the iniquitous situation wherein Japan is a vassal of Europe, particularly Britain. America and Japan must engage in trade that will rebound to the deep benefit of each. America must help Japan to improve. The United States must recognize the cultural glories of Japan yet be willing to show the Japanese the need for certain deep changes. Finally, America must greatly aid in bringing Christianity to Japan.[2]

Tokyo - In the fall of 1873, the prospect of war between Japan and China was real and increasing. Arriving in Japan, Bingham was eager to engage on the unequal treaty and Shimonoseki Indemnity issues. His supporters back home expected it. And his conscience demanded it. But the practice of diplomacy is more than simply defining and executing a plan. More often it is a matter of recognizing unexpected dangers and formulating a response. And so, from his first months in country, Bingham focused much of his energy on a looming international crisis, the possibility of armed confrontation between Japan and China. The issue was all the more delicate since there were Americans involved with the Japanese in making military preparations. Bingham understood the urgency of the immediate situation. He understood the dire consequences for America's interests in the larger Pacific region. And he understood the need for immediate action and how to proceed with that action.

While the Iwakura Mission was overseas, leaders who had stayed behind pushed for an aggressive approach to Japan's Asian neighbors. Plans had been drawn up and the Emperor had sanctioned a major invasion of Korea involving as many as 50,000 troops. The stated motive for the invasion was to avenge unacceptable slights from the Korean monarchy. These included the Korean kingdom's unwillingness to accept new diplomatic arrangements that would recognize the changed role of the Meiji Emperor. But Japan was also anxious to counter Russian encroachment in the neighborhood and a successful move into Korea would make a strong statement about Japanese intentions. The most prominent leader of the pro-invasion group was *Saigo Takamori* from the *Satsuma* Domain centered on Kagoshima, on Japan's southern island, Kyushu.

As soon as he returned from overseas, Iwakura took decisive steps to block the Korean invasion. The resulting confrontation between Iwakura and his supporters, most notably *Okubo Toshimichi*, and the Saigo group that had remained in Japan, created the first major internal crisis of the new Meiji Government.[3] When the Council of State met on September 13 and 14 to consider the proposed invasion, Okubo, who had accompanied the Iwakura Mission, spoke out against it. Okubo insisted that Japan must first devote itself to modernization. The expense of such an endeavor would be devastating, Okubo argued. Japanese leaders also worried that the government might have difficulty enforcing domestic order if unrest were to break out with much of its military outside the country.

Bingham's predecessor, Charles DeLong, had supported the group of Japanese officials favoring a Korea invasion. One year before the Council of State met and scrapped the idea of the invasion, DeLong had introduced Foreign Minister *Soejima Taneomi* to General Charles LeGendre. LeGendre was the American consul stationed at Amoy, China. In October of 1872, LeGendre was headed to Washington to lobby for a diplomatic assignment in Latin America. Amoy was across the strait from Taiwan (Formosa), and LeGendre had experience negotiating with indigenous Taiwanese natives. He had also advocated Japanese colonization of Taiwan as a way to pacify the island. In his view, the situation was analogous to America's treatment of native populations in the American West in those years.[4]

LeGendre had led an eventful life for years before he began his entanglement with John Bingham in 1874. Born in France in 1830, married in Brussels at age twenty-four to a New York heiress, LeGendre moved to the United States and became an American citizen. When the Civil War broke out, he joined the Union army and in 1862 was wounded in battle. He continued to serve and was under General Ulysses S. Grant at both Vicksburg and the Battle of the Wilderness, some of the heaviest fighting of the war. After suffering a severe facial wound, he became involved in recruitment and retired with the rank of brigadier general.[5]

Soejima agreed to hire LeGendre as a military advisor. With no approval from Washington, DeLong had placed the United States in a position of at least implied support for Japanese foreign military intervention.[6] When the faction led by Iwakura and Okubo stopped the Korea invasion, Saigo Takamori immediately resigned and headed back to Kagoshima. Okubo then reorganized the government, putting officials into positions of power who supported the go-slow approach on foreign intervention. Soejima retired as foreign minister and was replaced by *Terashima Munenori*[7]. Terashima had been educated in Europe and was minister to Great Britain when the Iwakura Mission visited that nation. With these moves, Okubo established himself as the most powerful individual in the administration.[8]

When the Meiji government's Council of State vetoed the plan for a Korea invasion, again gaining the Emperor's support, more aggressive forces turned to a separate plan, a plan which had already been under consideration. A smaller force had been organized in the summer of 1873 to sail to Taiwan to punish tribesmen for the murder there of castaways from a stranded *Ryukyu* fishing boat in 1871.[9] The proposed expedition raised delicate issues in Japan's relationship to China since both countries claimed control of the island chain which includes present day Okinawa. Acting to protect Ryukyu islanders would dramatically assert Japanese jurisdiction over the islands and call into question Chinese control over Taiwan.[10] LeGendre, already in the employ of the Japanese government, was busy helping Japan organize the Taiwan expedition.[11] The diplomatic community was concerned, particularly the British, with their long-cultivated contacts in the Meiji government and strong ties to the new Foreign Minister Terashima. In February, British Minister Sir Harry Parkes reported to London that a Japanese move into Taiwan might provoke war with China or even Russia. The British Foreign Ministry was less apprehensive than Parkes but still concerned.[12]

Bingham soon learned that final outfitting for the retaliatory expedition had begun and that LeGendre was very much involved. By April, rumors of the invasion were becoming a hot topic in the local English language press and Bingham passed these reports on to Secretary Fish.[13] Foreign diplomats were well aware of the critical divisions within the Japanese leadership. In a message dated April 22, Bingham reported that an American ship, *New York*, owned and operated by the Pacific Mail and Steam-Ship Company, was being hired to support the expedition. Bingham's report went on to say that two other Americans, United States Navy Lt. Commander Douglas Cassel and James Wasson, a West Point graduate working for the *Kaitakushi*[14], were joining the group. Wasson had a close personal relationship with his fellow West Point classmate, Frederick Grant, son of the President, a fact that was not lost on the American minister.[15] Wasson later figured prominently in Bingham's life in Japan when he became Bingham's son-in-law.

Bingham met with Terashima to clarify Japan's official position on the expedition and was reassured that Japan had no intention of going to war with China. Japan simply wanted to work with the Taiwanese aboriginals to arrange compensation and prevent future unfortunate incidents. Bingham replied that participation in such an action by Americans was not appropriate and handed Terashima his message which he asked the Japanese government to deliver to the American participants, discouraging their involvement in the mission. Bingham emerged from the meeting encouraged that the Taiwan expedition would not go forward. In a message to Fish dated April 24, 1874, he wrote that he was pleased to report that his representations had been successful and the mission was being suspended.[16] He was wrong.

The expedition was already underway. During the second week of April 1874, the first ships had already left *Shinagawa*, a port facility on Tokyo Bay just south of the capital. The expedition was headed first to Nagasaki. According to Edward House, an American reporter who accompanied the mission, before sailing, Cassel and Wasson had received messages "that contained a strong though not peremptory warning against joining the mission"[17] but the Americans "were not at all disposed to allow their good faith to be trifled away by a petulant interposition…"[18] In general, House was supportive of Bingham's approach to Japan and applauded Bingham's repeated declarations that America and other western nations should not impinge on Japan's independence. But in this instance, House saw the expedition as being well within Japan's rights. Any American intervention to prevent Japan from pursuing its independent foreign policy, House thought, amounted to meddling. And as far as Bingham's position was concerned, after all, House pointed out, the American minister had approved Cassel's leave of absence from American naval service to join the Japanese military.[19]

Washington, Tokyo, Amoy - By the time that Bingham's separate message warning that the mission was still ongoing arrived in Washington, the Japanese already had an organized military presence on the ground in Taiwan. In a message dated June 1, 1874, American consul in Amoy, J.J. Henderson, had reported that an estimated three thousand Japanese troops were there.[20] Just two days later, Henderson wrote informing Washington that he had been told by Chinese officials that it was common knowledge that Americans were taking part in what he termed "an invasion."[21] Then on June 6, Henderson issued a notification to American citizens saying the Chinese government had authority over Taiwan and that given America's treaty commitments to China, American citizens must withdraw from participating in any hostile action against China.

It was now obvious that Bingham's message of April 24 indicating suspension of the mission was outdated. The pace of communications had been overtaken by the speed of events. However, even during May, the American envoy's suspicions about the Japanese expedition had been growing. It was confirmed that Cassel and Wasson had proceeded with their participation. Bingham's intervention did result in withdrawing the important logistical support that the *New York* would have provided. Realizing that they needed to consider American discomfort with American citizens' participation, the Japanese authorities decided to keep LeGendre in Tokyo. On May 22, General *Saigo Tsugumichi*, in overall charge of the operation, landed in Taiwan with one thousand and five hundred additional troops[22]. On the same day, a Chinese naval contingent came into contact with the Japanese anchored off the coast. The Chinese insisted the Japanese were on Chinese territory and demanded the Japanese leave.

Saigo was not ready to end his mission. The next day Henderson received an official message from the Chinese, indicating they considered the Japanese actions unlawful and asserting full sovereignty over Taiwan and also the Ryukyu Islands. On June 5, S. Wells Williams, Charge d'affaires in Beijing, wrote to Consul Henderson in Amoy, saying that the Japanese "armed expedition" to Taiwan included American participants Cassel and Wasson who should be told immediately to desist. Williams did not specify how he had gotten the information about Cassel and Wasson. However, in a subsequent message from Williams two weeks later, Williams named Bingham as the source.[23]

Recognizing the separate communications between American posts in China and Japan could further confuse an already difficult situation, during May, Bingham had opened up communications directly with Williams.[24] With no minister at post in Beijing at the time, Williams, a China hand from the missionary community, was temporarily the senior American diplomat in China. Williams in Beijing had likely become aware of Bingham's concern about the American participants sometime during the latter part of May. On June 8, in a message to Washington, Consul General George Seward, serving in Shanghai, included a message sent to him earlier by Williams. Seward was a Lincoln appointee and nephew of former Secretary of State William Seward. Williams' message said that the Chinese Foreign Office had been under the misimpression that the *New York* was a man of war and that LeGendre was the leader of the Japanese expedition. Misimpression or not, the message could prove an irritant in the American relationship with China.[25] Bingham's relationship with Williams through missionary channels and his personal relationship with Seward and his family proved to be useful connections.

Bingham's assessments of Japanese intentions, and his private communications with Williams, were important elements in the development of the affair. It was also apparent that with Bingham's open opposition to the expedition, LeGendre's influence with the Japanese government declined rapidly.[26] Bingham did not argue that Japan had no right to conduct the retaliatory mission, nor did he question Japan's claim to the Ryukyu Islands. Bingham's sole expressed concern was that American citizens should not be involved. The timing of events, however, suggests that Bingham worked to block American participation in the expedition before the Chinese formally moved to claim that such participation contravened America's treaty obligations. Not only did America have a treaty with China but the Neutrality Act of 1794 prohibited Americans from waging war against any nation with which the United States was at peace. In April, Bingham had already called for recall of American advisors. This was well before a May letter to the American Legation from the Chinese government, claiming American citizens' participation contravened the 1858 Sino-U.S. treaty.[27]

Journalist Edward House was convinced that Bingham's uncharacteristic intervention in what House saw as a purely Japanese matter was due to Bingham's having been misled by a sensationalist press. Such reports, he thought, had overplayed the potential for war between Japan and China. House was appreciative of Japan's growing political maturity and sympathetic to her willingness to provide a service to the entire global shipping world by suppressing any violent activity by the Taiwanese tribes. He strongly criticized Bingham's interference which he believed was detrimental to building a strong bilateral relationship with Japan.

For House, the attempted interruption of the Taiwan expedition by the United States was symptomatic of western attitudes toward Japan. The following closing passage from House's 1875 recount of the incident, published in Tokyo in 1875 as *The Japanese Expedition to Formosa*, expresses his frustration about foreigners' condescending attitudes.

> *Why, then, is that place denied them? There are two equal explanations, which go far to answer the inquiry. The first lies in the universal ignorance of Western communities rejecting the character, the spirit, and the aspirations of the Japanese people. The second is found in the misapprehensions under which the Western Powers rest in regard to the actions of the government, which may be traced to the incorrect views held and thrust forward, sometimes in innocent though baleful error, sometimes with vicious and selfish design, by Ministers who represent in Japan what they understand to be the interest or necessities of their respective countries. The result is that Japan is commonly looked upon as a fantastic and amusing problem, a topic for occasional fanciful discussion, a distant and grotesque*

object, to be sometimes, perhaps indulgently caressed but never to be approached with candid convictions or serious sympathy. To one public she is a pet, to another a puzzle, to a third, a convenient victim. By all she is looked upon as a sort of toy nation; playing at progress and seeking to imitate the practices of genuine civilization simply as a diversion.[28]

Bingham's representations to the Japanese government only pertained to American citizens' participation in the expedition. In their messages both Bingham and Williams argued that it was lawful to prevent American citizens from being involved in hostile activities with a nation, in this case China, with which the United States had peaceful relations. Further, American treaty obligations superseded the individual's right to join a foreign army. As the dialog between and among Washington and Tokyo, Amoy and Beijing proceeded over the summer months, this legal point was discussed at length. In the end, the State Department concluded that LeGendre, Cassel, and Wasson had not violated United States law. As part of its arguments, the State Department cited the many soldiers from foreign countries who had joined the United States Army and fought in the Civil War and other conflicts.

As the debate over the legality of Americans' participation in the expedition raged, another melodramatic brushstroke was made to LeGendre's colorful career. Furious at being pulled back from the expedition, LeGendre had made his way to Amoy. On August 5, Henderson sent a telegram informing Seward in Shanghai that LeGendre had arrived in Amoy. Seward told Henderson to arrest LeGendre immediately and to await instructions from the Legation in Beijing.[29] After weeks in custody, the Civil War general was released when word of the State Department's exculpatory decision on the issue reached China.

Bingham had a number of reasons for handling the Taiwan expedition incident as he did. First, he was sensitive to the view from Washington regarding peace in the region. Provocations that might appear slight at first could easily trigger broader confrontation. Second, by informing a trusted confidant like Williams in China, Bingham understood that it was important to learn how American officials in China understood the situation. American interest should not be viewed solely from Japan. Third, Bingham was aware of LeGendre's reputation and saw the brash general as more adventurous than reliable.

Finally, Bingham's involvement in this affair did no harm to his relationship with the Japanese government. Rather, his support for the group of determined modernizers who prevailed in setting Japan's foreign policy of moderation proved advantageous. And he knew that new Foreign Minister Terashima was part of this group. The recall of the Taiwan expedition and the shelving of plans for a Korea invasion cemented the control of the faction that favored internal strengthening over external adventurism. As a result, the group of Meiji leaders that included Iwakura, *Ito Hirobumi* and Okubo Toshimichi came to dominate Japanese foreign policy. It is also important to note that both Ito and Okubo, as young men, had been students of Guido Verbeck, a leading missionary and a close associate of Bingham and David Thompson. The international crisis that unfolded just as Bingham had arrived in Japan "determined the nature of the Meiji government and its policies for the next two decades."[30]

In a message from Washington dated July 29, 1874,[31] Fish concurred with Bingham's handling of the affair and Bingham

56

passed the secretary's instructions to the consulate in Nagasaki, the American outpost closest to the events. In a follow-up message dated September 1, 1874,[32] Fish noted that Bingham had been given broad authority to do what he believed to be necessary to ensure American neutrality in any dispute between China and Japan. Secretary Fish also assured the American minister that President Grant was following these developments closely. In these communications, Fish clearly appreciated Bingham's professional handling of the issue, even if he might have thought some of the messages from Tokyo were longwinded and legalistic.

By early July, Japanese military operations were drawing to a close and talks had begun between Japan and China to find a broader resolution. Finally, on October 31, Japan and China agreed to a treaty and Japanese troops were set to leave by late December. The treaty called for China to recognize that the Japanese incursion into Taiwan was justified, China would pay an indemnity, and China would guarantee the safety of the sea-lanes around Taiwan. The expedition was a political success for the Japanese. Despite continued Chinese attempts to claim suzerainty over the Ryukyu Islands, Japanese administrative control remained firm. And American bilateral relations with both China and Japan survived largely unhurt.

The Chinese press had cheered LeGendre's arrest. Japan continued to appreciate his services. And by fall, China and Japan had reached an accommodation. For Minister Bingham, there were plenty of other issues to work on with the neophyte Meiji government. As for LeGendre, he remained in Japan in the private employ of *Okuma Shigenobu* until 1890, when he left for Korea to become an advisor to the Korean king, *Kojong*. In 1878, he published a tract, *Progressive Japan*, in which he argued for creation of a Japanese government that would strike a balance between Imperial authoritarianism and what he described as the mob rule of excessive democratic government.[33] Receiving a positive review in the *Japan Mail*, it is clear that LeGendre remained a presence in Tokyo's foreign community.[34] A free thinker on religious and social issues, it is unlikely that the straight-laced Bingham and the flamboyant LeGendre had much to do with each other.[35]

The events of late 1873 and early 1874 strengthened Bingham's fledgling relationship with Japan's most influential political faction. The coming years saw rebellion and assassination. But throughout this period, the consistency of individual relationships between Minister Bingham and the American Legation and Meiji government leaders was beneficial. Bingham now had a good platform from which to remind the Japanese that the United States could serve as a useful counterbalance against what he saw as the rapacious machinations of the European powers especially Great Britain.

CHAPTER SIX

Policy Engagement: Indemnity and Treaties

Tokyo - Despite his preoccupation with the Korean and Taiwan crises, the new American minister was able to begin to engage on two key diplomatic policy goals that were to define his career in Japan. These were return of the Shimonoseki Indemnity payment and repeal or revision of the unequal treaties. By resolutely addressing these issues, Bingham could keep himself in front of key groups of supporters back home. He also firmly believed that achieving these goals was morally right and practically smart, serving the mutual interests of the United States and Japan.

Shimonoseki, Tokyo and Washington - The Shimonoseki Indemnity agreement followed a military confrontation between western powers and the Choshu domain in western Honshu, Japan's largest island. In 1863, the Civil War was raging in the United States and the Tokugawa government had recently issued its charge to Expel the Barbarian (攘夷勅命 Sonno Joi). A small American vessel, the *Pembroke*, was fired upon by Choshu batteries while anchored for the night near the port of Shimonoseki. Damage was minimal and the *Pembroke* continued on to China. The Americans, however, did not let the incident go and were able to fix an indemnity of $11,200 for damages that the Japanese agreed to pay. The other western powers, particularly at the

French troops with captured Japanese cannons at Shimonoseki 1864. Public domain.

urging of Rutherford Alcock, the first British minister to be resident in Japan, decided that stronger action was merited. Joining with the French and the Dutch, the Americans and the British mounted an expedition to the Choshu coast, the fleet sailing from Yokohama in late August of 1864.[1] American Minister Robert Pryun was eager to join the combined effort with the European powers. It was important to demonstrate that the Union, not the Confederacy, was the government that was in control of American foreign policy as the Union and the Confederacy slugged it out on the battlefields back home. Pryun had few resources and was only able to charter a small steamer, the *Ta-kiang*, as the American contribution.[2]

The expedition successfully destroyed the Choshu shore batteries and the *daimyo* was forced to accept the foreigners' conditions. Although American damage was minimal, after some discussion the four powers agreed to set the Shimonoseki Indemnity at $3,000,000. Each nation was to be given an equal share of $750,000. The Tokugawa government, reeling from internal political dissention, assumed responsibility for payment.[3]

The military conflict was over, but the political wrangling had just begun. By the summer of 1866, the Japanese were making payments on the indemnity. But the Tokugawa government was wobbly; by November 1867, it had fallen. In early 1868 the Meiji Restoration was inaugurated. In the chaos of the transition, repayment of the indemnity was suspended. In time, the Meiji government did assume responsibility for repayment but asked that further disbursement be postponed until 1872.

Prodded by missionary, education and business constituencies in the States, critics of the Shimonoseki agreement argued that by demanding reparations far exceeding actual damages, the agreement was unjust and "unbecoming the character of the United States, as a just and generous people..."[4] A further concern was that the financial burden on Japan's government threatened the political stability of the new Meiji government. This was particularly undesirable at a time when Americans saw hopeful signs that Japan was moving in a direction where American interests might be more effectively cultivated.

Japan's representative in Washington, Minister *Mori Arinori*, who had studied in the United States shortly before the Meiji government took over, understood this mix of motivations well. Having established a close relationship with the secretary of state, Mori presented Hamilton Fish with an English language draft of a memorial he had prepared entitled *Religious Freedom in Japan*. He claimed that he intended to present the memorial to the Meiji government. The memorial had three pillars: matters of conscience must not be subject to force, government shall not impose religious beliefs on its citizens, and Japan should avoid instituting a state religion. Mori knew that any evidence of Japanese liberal thinking on religious issues was seductive to the American public. The memorial was published in English but never translated into Japanese. Fish replied to Mori with appreciation for the Japanese minister's points. Mori had reached his intended audience.[5]

Even before he had any idea that he would become minister to Japan, John Bingham was fully aware of this political effort. Many of his Republican friends in Congress were supporters of this cause. In March 1873, six months before Bingham was to arrive in Japan, Minister Mori presented a book he had prepared entitled *Education in Japan* to future president, Ohio congressman and Bingham associate, James Garfield. The book contained letters on educational philosophy from prominent American educators. It included a letter from Birdsey Northrup. During the next decade, Northrup became a prominent figure in both the educational and missionary communities, arguing against the Shimonoseki Indemnity. On campuses and in churches, interest in the indemnity issue was robust. This was a community that shared John Bingham's religious views and his political values.[6]

From 1866 until Bingham left for Japan in 1873, there was annual consideration of the Shimonoseki Indemnity issue, either in the Senate or the House. During the lame duck session of the 42nd Congress, Bingham's last months in the House of Representatives, the issue surfaced again. On January 20 and again on January 27, 1873, reports were entered into the record from groups asking for relief of the Japanese indemnity. On the earlier date the *Congressional Globe* (the current iteration of this publication is called the *Congressional Record*) noted the clerk's tabling of a petition on the indemnity repayment issue from the president and faculty of Ohio Wesleyan University. The petition was filed by Bingham's friend, James Garfield. Less than a week later, two petitions were filed supporting use of the indemnity for educational purposes in Japan. One was prepared and signed by Harvard President Charles W. Eliot and six Harvard professors. The other was signed by 452 college and local educational officials from dozens of schools in 24 states and the District of Columbia. It had been prepared and circulated by the faculty of Williams College, Garfield's alma mater.[7]

Washington, D.C. - American officials were very familiar with negotiations over indemnity payments. Two other recent cases had at least some relationship to the Shimonoseki Indemnity. These were agreements with Great Britain and with China. In the case of Great Britain, the United States demanded, and after long negotiations received, financial compensation for British involvement in allowing British naval yards to build ships for the Confederate Navy. These British-made ships had been used by the Confederates to harass and destroy Union maritime shipping. In Pacific waters, the most notable of the ships was the *Shenandoah*. The *Shenandoah* took as many as sixty prizes, many of them whalers, all but extinguishing that industry for America in the Pacific.[8] The Treaty of Washington, signed in 1872, among other items, contained a provision that Great Britain would pay an indemnity of $15,500,000 to the United States for damages to American merchant shipping. For Grant's top diplomat, Secretary of State Hamilton Fish, the treaty was the signal accomplishment of his tenure and marked a key milestone in America's relationship with Great Britain.[9]

The United States and the Chinese government had agreed that China would pay 600,000 *taels* or about $840,000 for damages to American property. The damages occurred during incidents related in part to French and British military encounters with the Chinese during the Second Opium War of 1856-1860.[10] In 1870, Senator Charles Sumner, whose career often entwined with John Bingham, gave a report in the Senate Foreign Relations Committee arguing that the indemnity funds should be used to support education in China. Sumner introduced a report by an eminent group of New York business and academic leaders that called for returning to China any surplus from the indemnity after payment of just claims. If China refused to accept the money, the United States would use the funds "in founding a literary institution for the equal benefit of Chinese and Americans."[11] The chairman of the committee of business leaders and academicians was Isaac Ferris, at the time Chancellor of New York University. Ferris was also a prominent clergyman of the Dutch Reformed Church and a corporate member of the American Board of Commissioners of Foreign Missions.[12] Senator Sumner also introduced a similar report from a group of Chicago leaders. Washington politicians and their constituencies interested in foreign affairs were well versed in indemnity issues. John Bingham knew many of these Washington politicians personally and represented constituencies with the same political sentiments.

Tokyo - Six weeks after presenting his credentials to Emperor Meiji and several days before a banquet for his departing predecessor, Charles DeLong, Bingham was approached by the British Minister, Sir Harry Parkes. Bingham reported to Secretary Fish that Sir Harry had requested American cooperation in sending a message to the Japanese government on the indemnity issue. The agreement in 1866, allowing the Japanese to postpone payments for three years, had been extended in 1869 for an additional three years. When that period expired in 1872, further discussions had been held but no actual payments had been made.[13] Parkes asked Bingham to join the other Ministers whose nations were party to the agreement to approach the Japanese with a strong demand to pay the remaining portion of the indemnity.

In his message to Fish, Bingham noted actions taken in the House of Representatives to end the indemnity payments and indicated he would not join Parkes' demarche.[14] In his reply, Fish wrote that although the House had taken action, the Senate had not. He added that the State Department did not intend to push the issue with the Senate. However, recognizing the sensitivity of the political atmosphere around the issue and Bingham's personal feelings, Fish said the Legation did not need to accede to Parkes' demand. Still, Parkes continued to insist. British influence prevailed on the Japanese government and the Japanese began to make payments.

At first these payments were made in small installments. Bingham reported to Fish in a message dated February 23, 1874, that Parkes had approached him with respect to a payment of $5,833.33 from the Japanese. The minister further informed Fish that in the absence of specific instructions from the Department, he would not accept the money.[15] In his reply, Fish directed Bingham to accept the money, and Bingham complied. By late summer, after some grousing about how the payment was being carried out, Bingham informed Fish that the account had been settled and could be closed pending Fish's approval to do so. Fish did so.

The account was closed but the issue was dormant, not dead. Bingham continued to advocate with the State Department for return of the money to the Japanese. From time to time he reminded the Department that there were still voices in Washington and the press continued to speak out on the issue. In a January 1875 message, Bingham reminded Fish that President Grant had spoken in favor of using the indemnity fund to support education in Japan.[16]

In the case of the Japanese incursion into Taiwan, Bingham had shown initiative. He had reacted quickly and because he understood the political context in both Washington and Tokyo, his actions were effective. The Shimonoseki Indemnity issue, by contrast, was not amenable to solution by Bingham in Tokyo. He understood how the issue played in the halls of Congress. But from across the Pacific, it was impossible for him to generate enough urgency to get the American government to pay attention to an issue that was peripheral to American politics. But Bingham had long since learned that patience could also be an effective political strategy. Hamilton Fish would not be secretary of state too much longer.

Washington, D.C - By the time of the Grant Administration, in the words of historian Marlene Mayo, America did not have a coherent policy but rather, "… a cluster of attitudes toward East Asia." [17] This lack of coherence is evidenced in treatment of the treaty issue by the administration in Washington. Before Bingham had left Congress, the issue had already surfaced on Capitol Hill. In 1872, leadership of the powerful American Board of Commissioners for Foreign Missions wrote to President Grant, asking for his support for revising the unequal treaties with Japan.[18] On December 2 of the same year, in his annual address to Congress, Grant called for treaty revision. As he arrived in Japan Bingham was hopeful that the issue could be moved through the Congress.

However odious the unequal treaties were for the Japanese, they did not violate two cardinal principles of America's Pacific policy that had been outlined decades earlier by Daniel Webster. These principles were no acquisitions of territory and open trade for all nations.

However, preoccupied by momentous domestic developments, the administration of President James Buchanan from 1857 to 1861, showed little interest in Asia. The principles were simply irrelevant. And then with the outbreak of the American Civil War, the presence of the United States in Japan shrunk to a few traders and missionaries. The latter group had first become active, particularly in the Yokohama area, as the decade of the 1850s drew to a close. In 1865, British Minister Parkes, a voluble personality and an experienced Asia hand, began his storied tour in Tokyo. Parkes' personality coupled with the overwhelming naval superiority of Great Britain in that part of Asia, cemented British dominance over foreign relations with Japan.

For William Seward, secretary of state under Lincoln and Andrew Johnson, foreign policy toward Asia promised a rendezvous with America's moral destiny. Seward's grand conception fit well with his Whig and subsequent Republican beliefs in promoting domestic infrastructure development and facilitating the overseas expansion of American business. But as secretary of state in wartime, Seward's main concern was to maintain good relations with the European powers. As far as Japan was concerned, this meant adherence to the Cooperative Policy and support of the unequal treaty system. To the State Department, the Cooperative Policy, which committed the United States to act in concert with the other western powers in Japan, confirmed the primacy of America's European relationships over those with Japan. In accordance with this, the United States joined the European nations in signing on to the Convention of 1866. This agreement entailed revisions to the unequal treaties with tariff terms particularly favorable to British interests.

One provision of the Convention provided for a five percent cap on tariffs, allowing Japan little leeway to protect its own nascent industries with higher duties. During the 19th century, tariffs were an important source of government revenue in many countries, accounting for the lion's share of many governments' tax collections. Fixing tariffs at such a low level favored European traders and impoverished the Japanese treasury. Such a low tariff policy was a direct contrast with Webster and Seward's economic policies as applied to America's domestic economy. It also weakened non-Western nations' ability to use trade policy to increase their own wealth and gain a measure of independence in their commercial relations with the West.

Tokyo - By 1868, another new factor had become important in America's relationship with Japan. This was the influence of missionaries, particularly those representing Protestant denominations that were influential at the time in American politics. The first group of prominent American missionaries, sponsored by the Presbyterian and Dutch Reformed Churches, included Dr. James C. Hepburn. Arriving first in 1859, Hepburn and his wife Clara were followed soon by Samuel Robbins Brown, Guido Verbeck and Dr. Duane Simmons. All four men went on to play major parts in Japan's response to the western intrusion. The Civil War had squeezed church donations for mission activities. But with the end of the war, a fresh wave of Christians of various denominations became active, most notably, in the Yokohama area. Many were graduates of elite American universities; Hepburn was a Princeton graduate and received his medical degree from the University of Pennsylvania. And the mission boards back in the United States were well connected to American political elites.

In general, the missionaries were more sympathetic than the business community to the Japanese animosity to the unequal treaties. And they were particularly dissatisfied with the provisions of the treaties that proscribed internal travel beyond Japan's extraterritorial enclaves. This feeling became more acute as the Meiji government began moving toward removal of the ban on proselytizing. And although the Cooperative Policy remained State Department diktat, Bingham was well aware of the missionaries' general dislike of the unequal treaties. He had strong political connections to the denominations most active in Japan at the time and understood well that political support for retaining the Cooperative Policy had eroded.

During the first months of his tenure in Japan, Bingham took energetic steps to encourage Washington to take action on treaty revision. In messages to the State Department, often with lengthy reports attached, he emphasized that if Japan were to open its interior to foreign participation, the potential for development would be substantial. Reflecting his experience in Congress representing a district where sheep herding was an important industry, in one message he passed along an abstract on raising cattle and sheep in undeveloped areas of Japan. Bingham estimated that with the proper growth strategy, Japan should be able to support an increase in its own population from the then current 30 million to three times that number.[19] Having in his lifetime watched the westward movement by European-American settlers into America's continental interior, Bingham was confident that the same type of pioneering spirit that had "settled" the American West would enrich Japan. A wealthier Japan would be a better market and partner for the United States. Japan would also be able to push back more forcefully against the threat from European colonial competitors, particularly Britain, and in the case of Japan's northern areas, Russia. For this to happen, Bingham argued, Japan's control over its own customs processes was imperative.

Secretary of State Hamilton Fish was more exasperated than

enthusiastic towards Bingham's initiatives. Preoccupied with other issues and unaware of "the significance of this period in the history of the Japanese people," Fish offered Bingham no encouragement. The State Department did not intend to push for revision or repeal of the treaties. [20] Failing to get support from Fish, the minister turned to President Grant, writing directly to the president, asking him to please prod the secretary for a response to his messages.[21] This effort also failed. By the time that Bingham had been appointed to the Japan post, Fish and Grant had established a firm working relationship. Their wives had become close friends and were often seen together on the Washington social scene.[22] When Grant left office he and his wife stayed with Fish and his wife for three weeks, Grant had even entertained the idea that Fish would be an able successor to the presidency.[23]

Bingham's relationship with Grant was marked by cordial, mutual respect. He did not expect that his appeal to Grant over the head of Fish would have changed Washington's stance on Japan and the Cooperative Policy. But he did know that the voices calling for revision or repeal of the treaties were supporters he wanted to cultivate. And early in his tenure in Tokyo he still retained at least some ambition for resuming elective office back home. Treaty revision would require Senate action. Few diplomats understood as well as Bingham how laborious it could be to get Senate concurrence. But he also knew the importance of keeping the issue alive and in chipping away piece by piece at the attitudes and behaviors that kept an unwanted policy in place. Success, experience had taught him, could come in installments. He had taken important steps to advance his goal of gaining repeal or revision of the unequal treaties among Washington's leaders. Support was insufficient but Bingham had helped bring attention to the need for change.

CHAPTER SEVEN

Gaining Foreign Community Support

Tokyo - In addition to backing from Washington policy makers, to be successful in achieving his intended goals in Japan, Bingham also needed to cultivate a working relationship with his fellow diplomats. Among this group were prickly personalities who had their own channels to Japanese leaders and even to Washington. Bingham's skill in navigating these complex currents enabled him to earn a broader appreciation and gradual acceptance of American policy positions. An example early in his tenure that earned respect from his European peers was his handling of Japan's regulations for hunting by foreigners.

Before Bingham's arrival, Minister DeLong had sent a message to Secretary Fish, detailing the Meiji government's measures to restrict hunting by foreign residents. The Japanese said the intent of the rules was to protect villagers and precincts near temples and shrines. The State Department, responding to DeLong's inquiry but now addressing Bingham, asked the newly arrived minister to examine the regulations to see if they violated Japan's bilateral treaty obligations.[1] Bingham provided his analysis which determined that the regulations did not contravene Japan's commitments.[2] In response, Secretary of State Fish concurred with Bingham adding the clarification that if there were an alleged violation of the regulations by an American citizen, that citizen was to be tried in the American consular court.[3]

For once, the American Legation and the Department in Washington were in agreement. But the British were not. In November, Bingham informed Fish that the British Minister, Sir Harry Parkes, insisted "...that the government of Japan cannot enact laws for the government of British subjects without the approval of the British representative; in other words, the laws passed by Japan were not to be observed, nor regarded as obligatory by British subjects..."[4] Bingham, careful constitutional lawyer that he was, argued that he possessed no authority to legislate over American citizens in the establishment of any regulations.

Sir Harry, by personality, experience, and circumstance, was the dominant figure in the foreign community. He had already clashed with his American counterpart over the collection of the Shimonoseki Indemnity payment. Disagreement over hunting regulations was a further irritant between the two men. That summer, a separate incident occurred that made the relationship even more difficult. Bingham had failed to join the other diplomatic representatives in criticizing handling by Japanese authorities of a dispute over the arrest of a Japanese employee of a British diplomat. The Japanese had entered the British Legation, an action the British argued violated the treaty agreement.[5] The strained relationship between the two men became a major topic in the small and ingrown foreign diplomatic community and even reached distant diplomatic circles.

Thirteen years younger than Bingham and having served in East Asia for thirty years, Parkes was a strong advocate of the treaty system and British commercial and legal prerogatives. Sir Harry, along with his elegant and sociable wife, Fanny, provided a beguiling contrast to the reserved and sometimes aloof Bingham family. The vivacious

Lady Fanny Parkes was the first foreign woman to climb Mt. Fuji. By contrast, Amanda Bingham's days were spent at home or with church friends. Parkes was known to have a temper. His deputy, Ernest Satow, who would return to Japan as Great Britain's Minister in 1895, even in his private personal diary, criticized Sir Harry carefully and in the Japanese *hiragana* syllabary which Parkes was not be able to read.[6] Sir Harry may have been charming, but risking his displeasure was not a good idea.

In August of 1874, Fish wrote to Bingham to let him know that complaints from the British and Russian governments had reached Washington from foreign capitals. The American minister was accused of being unwilling to join the other treaty powers in signing a document addressed to the Japanese government concerning the arrest of the Japanese servant involved in the domestic dispute with a British official.[7] Bingham informed Fish that the note had been hastily drafted and that since he resided in Tokyo while the rest of the diplomatic community remained in Yokohama, he had not been asked to review or sign the document. Fish accepted Bingham's explanation. Still, the strained relationship between the American minister and his European colleagues, amplified by the pro-British slant of the English language treaty port press, made it clear that Bingham had become a very weak link in the Cooperative Policy chain. That European diplomats could raise complaints directly with the secretary back in Washington was a reminder of the vulnerability of diplomats to gossip in the capital. But Bingham's ability to withstand these attacks can only have enhanced his standing as a minister with solid support back home. Such support helped raise his influence among his peers. It also was not lost on Japanese officials.

As the heat on the hunting issue began to diminish, it was Parkes who was isolated and Bingham who rallied the foreign representatives in Japan to an agreed compromise. In order to avoid direct submission of foreign treaty port residents to Japanese law, Bingham devised a license system. When purchasing a hunting license, the foreign hunter would also agree to certain restrictions printed on the license. Any violation, then, was not breach of Japanese laws or regulations but rather a contravention of stipulations agreed to at time of purchase of the license. The violator would be subject to damages determined by his own country's consular court. A broad outline of the compromise was contained in a message from Bingham to Fish sent toward the end of the year.[8] A clarification from Washington said that any American deemed in violation of the regulations could remit fines only to the American consular court, not the Japanese government.[9] The hunting controversy ended not with a bang but a whimper.

Bingham's deftly devised compromise was acceptable to the Japanese government and the foreign community. As a diplomat, in addition to keeping his home constituents satisfied, he had to appease a diverse diplomatic contingent and earn the support of an opaque host government. Significantly, as each legation published directions to their citizens on following the new regulations, only the American announcement made "direct allusion to the law of Japan and state that the citizens to whom the proclamation is addressed are expected to obey this law."[10] Bingham had made an important legal point reinforcing the validity of the Japanese law, and those in the foreign community who paid attention to such matters understood.

On several other issues as well, the United States had little quarrel with the Europeans. The issue of Japanese government issuance of passports for foreign nationals to travel outside the restricted treaty port areas is one such case. Before being replaced by Bingham, Minister

DeLong had written to Secretary Fish to inform the State Department of new regulations being issued by the Japanese concerning travel of foreigners into the interior of the country. Neither Bingham nor Fish had reservations about the authority for the Japanese to issue these regulations. The distinction between foreign authority in the treaty ports and Japanese authority beyond them was clear in the treaty. But for the Americans, the issue of most concern was that money should not be handled by Legation or consular officials. To accommodate this concern, a proviso was included that the Japanese government, not the consulates or the Legation, would be the repository of fees collected for these domestic passports.[11]

The contrast between the American and British positions on Japanese authority to legislate for foreign residents was significant and a major fault line in the Cooperative Policy. Bingham was able to exploit this difference by pointing out to the Japanese the greater respect America showed for Japanese authority. Still, this was at best a minor gain since the extraterritorial system and lack of control over customs policy remained in place as firmly as before. The Japanese government continued to find it impolitic to arouse the British lion or complain officially about the treaty system. It was not until Fish left office with the end of the Grant administration and a new secretary of state took office that Bingham was able to take important steps forward in his campaign for treaty revision.

Tokyo – In addition to commercial support, there were other communities, including the missionaries who were close to Bingham. During his first years in Japan, Bingham established a pattern of siding with Japan's right to legislate in areas affecting foreigners in matters not specifically excluded by the unequal treaties. His position on Japan's press laws was an exception to this pattern. In 1876, when the Japanese government promulgated new laws prohibiting foreign ownership or operation of Japanese language journals, and restricting anti-government statements in those journals, Sir Harry Parkes distributed the law to the British community in order to solicit compliance. By contrast, Bingham sent David Thompson's translation of the law to Secretary Fish with the comment that the law violated foreigners' treaty rights and asked for Department guidance. It was a reversal of each man's pattern, Parkes' affirming Japan's right to legislate where British citizen's rights were involved and Bingham's questioning Japan's right to do so in this case. In his reply to Bingham, Fish supported Japan's right to restrict non-Japanese from enjoying rights accorded to Japanese citizens.[12]

Bingham accepted Fish's instruction and did not continue to push the matter. But it is interesting to see why Bingham may have reversed his established position on this one issue. One writer has suggested that Bingham's experience as a champion of civil liberties had been a motivating factor in the minister's reversal.[13] A second possible consideration in Bingham's thinking was his intention to show sympathy for the missionary position on the issue. In preparing his translation of the Press Law, missionary and Legation interpreter, Thompson, certainly discussed the law's contents and potential impact with Bingham. In a case that had come up several months earlier, Japanese officials had questioned an American missionary about distribution of two religious tracts, an action that Bingham argued fell within the treaty rights.[14] For the missionaries in Japan, getting "the Word" out to Japanese in the Japanese language was vital. Given his close friendships in the missionary community, Bingham appreciated this concern. But when Fish instructed Bingham not to advocate against the Press Law, the minister complied without complaint. Several years later Bingham accepted further press restrictions, restrictions that extended to the English language press. This indicates Bingham understood Fish's position, even if he had argued the opposite to placate his missionary colleagues in the past. Although the policy he was advocating was unlikely to prevail, it was good politics to show support to his constituents. Bingham was, after all, a politician and a successful one at that.

In Washington, America's approach to Japan remained inconsistent. But in addressing the key issues of return of the Shimonoseki Indemnity, revision of the unequal treaties, and less important but related concerns, Bingham had begun to influence America's policy direction and to steer the process to concrete and specific goals. He understood the personalities and practices that moved issues in Washington. Early in his tenure in Japan it was clear to both the Japanese government and the foreign community that America now had a representative in Tokyo who had both the intention and the ability to move America from the periphery to the center of diplomacy in the Pacific.

Chapter Eight

Decent and in Good Order with an Exception

Tokyo - John Bingham was an experienced lawyer and a celebrated legislator; now, he had to become a manager. The American mission to Japan consisted of the Tokyo Legation, the Yokohama Consulate General, and consulates in Hakodate in the north, Nagasaki in the south, and Kobe in central Japan. He rapidly put the Tokyo Legation in good order but struggled throughout his years in Japan with a difficult personal relationship with Consul General Thomas Van Buren in Yokohama.

Tsukiji – Bingham recognized that an upgrade of the Legation's physical presence was important, both symbolically and practically as evidence of America's commitment to the bilateral relationship. When he first arrived, the new minister had no appropriate place to live or work and no functioning staff. The formal American Legation was a converted temple, *Zenpukuji*, in what were then the southern suburbs of Tokyo. The original structure on site had been occupied by Townsend Harris when he was negotiating America's treaty with the Tokugawa government. Its main building had burned down and then was rebuilt. Charles DeLong felt the building, which he called the "paper-house legation" was inadequate and certainly not appropriate for a residence for his family. Furthermore, it was unsafe.[1] Both DeLong and his

American Legation, Azabudai, Tokyo from American Embassy Tokyo website.

predecessor, Robert Van Valkenburgh, had lived in a house on lot 27 on the Bluff in Yokohama and traveled to Tokyo to conduct business with the central government.[2] Bingham recognized that remaining in Yokohama was not workable. He needed to reside and work in Tokyo to deal effectively with the Japanese government. He acted quickly to find an appropriate property in Tokyo where his family could live and where the American mission to Japan could operate.

To do that Bingham had to solve two problems. He had to find a site and he had to find a way to pay for it. The first was the easier problem to solve. The land at Tsukiji was marshy and boasted the least fragrant neighborhoods in the city. But the location, not far from Meiji government offices and near the Tokyo terminal of the recently opened rail connection with Yokohama, was convenient. Tsukiji's growing concentration of western residents and the relocation of fellow Cadizian David Thompson just months before Bingham's arrival made the area seem even more attractive. Not ideal and decidedly not picturesque, Tsukiji was at least adequate for a residence and legation office. Bingham had found a site for the Legation.

The next problem was money. Some diplomats sent abroad by the American government were wealthy and able to subsidize their own service. John Bingham was not one of those. With no funding from Washington and limited resources of his own, Bingham worked with the State Department and with an American businessman with property in Tsukiji to rent and furnish property for a residence and an office.[3] By the end of the year, funding had come through from Washington, and Bingham signed a two-year lease at $4,500 per year in February, 1874. From Bingham's own annual salary of $12,000, the Minister paid $800 per year as his private share of the housing expenses.

By March, the Bingham family moved out of Yokohama and into the new facilities at Tsukiji. All that remained was to dispute the Yokohama hotel bill and borrow money to furnish the new office and living quarters. An experienced attorney and a thrifty individual, Bingham saw to the hotel bill dispute himself. To furnish the rented property, he received a loan from Horace Capron, who headed up the largely American-led *Kaitakushi*.[4]

Bingham's relationship with Capron dated back to his years in Washington, D.C., when Capron had served as commissioner of agriculture. The case of the Hokkaido Development Department, *Kaitakushi*[5] and the hiring of Horace Capron provide an interesting study of the quirks in Japan's recruitment of foreign experts. American advisors were prominent in education and other areas such as shipping, but their single most concentrated contingent was in the *Kaitakushi*. During the period May 1871 to May 1875, thirty-one Americans were employed with this organization, which was charged with designing and executing a strategy to develop Japan's northern island of Hokkaido.[6]

When Bingham arrived in Japan in 1873, there were fewer than 70,000 Japanese living on Hokkaido along with perhaps 15,000 Ainu aboriginals. In 1869, the last remnants of Tokugawa forces, who had fled north to Hokkaido to make a last stand against the new Meiji regime, were defeated. The same year the *Kaitakushi* was created. The Meiji government was eager to demonstrate control over the territory, particularly since the Russians were active in the neighborhood. The *Kaitakushi* was put under the control of General *Kuroda Kiyotaka*, who had led the Meiji government troops in the final rout of the remnants of daimyo resistance. Recognizing the need for foreign expert development assistance and favoring the United States as a potential supplier of that expertise, Kuroda traveled to Washington, D.C. in 1871. He had authorization to interview and hire appropriate experts for the organization.

The Kuroda delegation's meeting with the commissioner of agriculture had immediate and positive results. Accompanied by his friend and fellow Satsuma native, Mori Arinori, who had only recently arrived in Washington as Japan's first minister, Kuroda met with Commissioner Horace Capron. Kuroda and Mori hoped Capron could recommend experts to help staff the *Kaitakushi*. Capron was an important figure in Washington's political world, but he was not a full cabinet member. The Agriculture Commission had been established in 1862 and Capron, as its head, received an annual salary of $3,000. Rather than assist the Japanese in finding candidates, Capron, in his mid-sixties at the time, decided to take on the assignment himself. No doubt he was encouraged by the $10,000 salary plus transportation to and from Japan and housing and other benefits while there. By the time Bingham arrived in Japan, Capron had already become a very visible figure in the limited foreign social circles.[7]

Capron shared Bingham's negative view of the British and their role in Japan. He complained about intrepid traveler Isabella Bird's characterization of Hokkaido and the Ainu. He scoffed at British dismissal of the agricultural potential of Japan's northern island and dismissed British attitudes toward Japan and her progress.[8] Capron had established a solid relationship with leading Japanese politicians, making him an important ally as Bingham began to build his own crucial contacts in the Meiji government. In his personal diary on March 1, 1874, Capron wrote, "Arranged to let our minister's representative have some $4000 to $5000 to enable him to fit up his house sufficient for his family and offices."[9] Capron's loan was key in getting the Legation established. Both the loan and Capron's access to and knowledge of Japan's key leaders were valuable assets to the newly arrived Bingham.

In addition to finding a place to live and a place to work, the new minister had to hire a staff. Durham Stevens, who arrived with Bingham, was eager and hard-working but had little knowledge of Japan and the Japanese language. Bingham's predecessor, Charles DeLong had an interpreter who had worked with him, Nathan Rice. But Bingham found Rice to be dissolute and an embarrassment to the mission.[10] Bingham turned to fellow Cadizian and Presbyterian missionary David Thompson to fill the interpreter slot. Given the restrictions on proselytization enforced by the Japanese government, it was not unprecedented for missionaries to take employment outside the church.[11] In China as well, missionaries had served in diplomatic positions. But within the small Presbyterian missionary group in Japan, Bingham's approach to Thompson was controversial.

David Thompson's wife Mary, née Mary Parke, had arrived in Japan in 1872. An 1866 graduate of Xenia Female Seminary in Ashland, Ohio, she had worked as a schoolteacher before applying to the Board of

Foreign Missions for an overseas posting. Married in 1874 in Japan, the young couple discussed whether it would be proper for David to take the interpreter position.[12] The offer of the interpreter's position and whether Thompson should accept it, split the small Presbyterian missionary community. And as any good missionary couple would, the Thompsons prayed for divine guidance. The Presbyterian missionaries in Tokyo and Yokohama did exactly what any Presbyterian group, a denomination fiercely proud of its democratic governing procedures, would have done. They held a meeting and then took a vote.[13] While the Thompsons prayed and the mission community squabbled, Bingham went ahead with the hiring process.[14] Finally, on December 31, 1874, Thompson's commission to serve as interpreter arrived from Washington.[15]

In the same month that Thompson received notification of his commission, the British mission moved into impressive quarters in *Ichibancho*, overlooking the Imperial Palace moat, real estate the British Embassy continues to occupy today. As the new year of 1875 began, John Bingham's British counterpart, Sir Harry Parkes, had a staff of at least a dozen including well-trained and experienced professional British foreign service officers, a mounted guard and facilities and funds for diplomatic entertainment. Bingham understood Congress as well as any previous minister to Japan. His service on the House committee that oversaw the State Department's budget even gave him an appreciation of the details of the process. He was fully aware that the American Legation would not be able to approach Britain's imperial trappings. But now he had a home, an office, an important colleague, and a small but dedicated staff. To his Calvinist satisfaction, the American Legation in Tokyo was "decent and in good order."[16] At the other terminus of the railway to Yokohama, things were not so orderly.

30 P 6

Legation and Minister's Residence Tsukiji, Library of Congress.

Yokohama - Despite the national responsibility inherent in the ministerial position, Bingham's managerial control of the consulates, America's posts in other cities of Japan, was tenuous. This was partly due to the slowness of communications. But it also resulted from an institutional weakness in the staffing of overseas missions. Appointments to consular positions were made by the president. Consuls did not need to clear or coordinate their messages to Washington through the minister, who was accredited to the host government and posted in the capital of the host country. Because of its proximity to the capital and the social intermingling of the Tokyo and Yokohama foreign communities, the relationship between the Consulate General of Yokohama and the Legation in Tokyo was quite different from that of the more far-flung consulates at Nagasaki, Hakodate and Kobe. As consul general, the head of the Yokohama operation was the first among equals of the subordinate consulates. A consul or consul general with his own ambitions and with a coterie of supporters at home and in Washington could create significant mischief. Consul General Van Buren in Yokohama did just that.

Van Buren had a political pedigree, wealthy friends, and significant character weaknesses. Born in 1824, Thomas Brodhead Van Buren was the son of Dr. Peter Van Buren, a cousin of President Martin Van Buren. Thomas married Harriet Sheffield in 1853. Harriet was the daughter of Joseph Sheffield who provided funds and property to establish the Sheffield Scientific School at Yale University. In his early career, Sheffield had become a successful shipper of cotton from Gulf of Mexico ports, and by the 1840's and 1850's had become a successful railroad builder in New England and the Midwest.[17] Appointed by President Grant as a Commissioner to the Vienna Exhibition of 1873, Thomas Van Buren left that assignment under a cloud, according to press reports from Englewood, New Jersey, where he lived and owned a large farm.[18] Relying on political and family connections, he emerged from this scandal as consul general based in Yokohama, once again appointed by President Grant. Van Buren arrived to take up his post six months after Bingham assumed the minister position. It was a foreign service trope at the time, and still is, that often some of the most difficult personalities are assigned to the posts farthest from Washington.

In his initial communications with Bingham, Van Buren's tone seemed gracious and even ingratiating, a collegiality that Bingham did not reciprocate. Van Buren's personal background of East Coast privilege contrasted with Bingham's austere Midwestern reserve. With his clear but often legalistic approach to issues, Bingham soon found Van Buren to be lazy and incompetent. Then, toward the end of 1874, all hell broke loose. In a private letter dated November 24, 1874, Van Buren wrote to Bingham apologizing for a visit his wife, Harriet, had made to the minister and declaring, "She is unquestionably insane and has been so for years."[19]

The immediate cause of this outburst was a conversation at the dinner table in the consul general's home in Yokohama. At the dinner, Van Buren's wife reportedly accused Mrs. Denison, wife of Van Buren's assistant, Henry Denison, of being seen inappropriately around town with an officer of a visiting American naval vessel. Claiming his wife always attacked the ones with whom he is most friendly, Van Buren wrote that this time Harriet had chosen Mrs. Denison as her victim. Rambling on, Van Buren wrote that his wife had an appetite for stimulants which he tried to keep under lock and key. He also accused the naval officer of slandering the Van Buren family. In another long letter penned less than a week later, Van Buren again apologized but not for his own behavior. He regretted that his wife had dragged Bingham and the minister's family into this affair. Van Buren was certainly distraught when he wrote both these letters and the deteriorating handwriting, particularly in the long second letter, argued that he was not entirely sober, a condition not at odds with numerous other descriptions of the consul general's behavior.[20]

During the following weeks, there were continued exchanges of letters that mentioned conversations between and among the parties involved. Van Buren wrote to Mr. Denison. Mrs. Van Buren wrote to Bingham – two letters in two days.[21] Mrs. Van Buren wrote to Mr. Denison on February 15 saying that although I am fond of you, Mr. Denison, your wife "has by her conduct, openly proclaimed herself my enemy."[22] The same day Van Buren wrote to Bingham, complaining that Bingham's daughters were ignoring him at social functions. Van Buren claimed this was an affront to his position as consul general.[23] Then on that same day, February 15, Harriett Van Buren's father began writing a letter to John Bingham. The ruckus had reached New Haven.

Writing just months before his 82nd birthday, Joseph Sheffield demonstrated where his daughter got her energy if not her sense of judgment. The papers Bingham left behind in his home in Cadiz after his death are not a complete record of his lifetime professional correspondence. Many he kept for purely personal or sentimental reasons. Others are financial records or correspondence that might have sensitive private information. Among these is a lengthy letter from Van Buren's father-in-law. Portions of the letter follow:

February 15, 1875

Hon: John A. Bingham,
Yedo --- Japan

My Dear Sir,

I am compelled to take the liberty of addressing you, and of asking your friendly advice in behalf of my ill and much distressed daughter, Mrs. Van Buren, now in Yokohama;
...

My daughter needs advice and sympathy in her unhappy position, being about to give up further attempts to live with a man who has treated her so ill for so many years, ...

...I have marked this strictly private, and now wish you, after you have read it carefully, if you will do me the favor to do so, to commit it to the flames:

..., in Vienna... he got into such a muddle and disgraced the country, or rather gave Mr. Jay the opportunity to do so. In that affair at Vienna his wife, like the true woman

she is, clung to him...

...all our friends made great efforts to save him from utter disgrace by getting the administration to give him some appointment, however unimportant, and Mr. Fish from purest friendship to me..., finally succeeded in getting him nominated for the position he now fills [and which I very much fear he will disgrace before he leaves it]

...

For the sake of introducing his daughter favorably to what little good society there is at present in Yokohama, she has, whenever the state of her health would permit, accepted all invitations and with cheerful countenance tho with a bleeding heart has endeavored to disguise her situation and unhappily (sic). She asks me to write to you, there being no American lawyer in Yokohama, that if they shall agree on terms of separation she may have someone in whom she has confidence to consult with, and advise her and draw up proper papers.

...I might have mentioned that his associations and habits and "indulgences" are altogether more open in Yokohama than they were in New York and have already attracted the notice of many of the better folk in Yokohama.[24]

Sheffield continued and then finished writing for the day. Reading over what he had written the next morning, he added two pages recounting Van Buren's military record during the Civil War, charging that whenever the consul general's unit appeared to be about to engage in battle, Van Buren arranged to be either on leave or to get sick. Also, enclosed in his letter to Bingham, Sheffield included a letter of credit to pay for Harriett's passage back to New Jersey, assuming her husband would refuse to provide money to her.

Bingham forwarded her father's letter to Harriet Van Buren who then informed the minister that she had not told her husband about the letter and begged Bingham not to let the letter become public. Late in March, Mrs. Van Buren wrote to Bingham, accusing Mrs. Denison of continuing to circulate scandals. At the end of June, in preparation for Independence Day, the consul general wrote his minister and explained that he and his wife had planned a celebration for the 4th of July, had invited the Binghams, and Mrs. Denison as well, and had suggested the Binghams spend the night at his residence. Alleging that Bingham had given his "cordial assent" to this plan to use the inspiration of the day to lay aside differences, Van Buren then said that he now is in receipt of a letter of regret from the minister and an invitation to an event hosted at the Legation. "Under the circumstances," Van Buren wrote, "your invitation is a gratuitous insult to which I did not think you would lend yourself."[25]

In a letter to Secretary of State Hamilton Fish dated August 12, 1875, an anonymous writer signed "American" complained about how the "unsophisticated Binghams" have been fooled by the ambitious schemes of a certain woman.[26] The Secretary forwarded the letter back to Bingham, asking if he might be able to determine the author by the handwriting. Van Buren's assistant, Henry Denison, confirmed the handwriting to be Mrs. Van Buren's. Denison explained to the Minister that "in Yedo and Yokohama it is considered rather a slight rather than otherwise not to be slandered by Mrs. Van Buren; and, as you very well know, not a single respectable American lady in Yokohama or Yedo of any social standing has escaped her vituperation."[27]

By the end of the year, Mrs. Van Buren came up to Tokyo to meet with Bingham, presumably to pick up the letter of credit for her transpacific return passage. And then on March 8, 1876, Thomas Van Buren sent a peace offering to John Bingham, "a dozen bottles of good sherry," begging Bingham to accept.[28] Bingham promptly replied, writing "In view of our official relations I deem it my duty to decline respectfully" the gift of sherry.[29] The curtain had come down on the first of several acts of the minister and consul general's melodrama, a window into the personalities and mores of Bingham's time and place. The Van Buren melodrama had paused but not ended.

As minister, Bingham had to surmount considerable management obstacles. His control over budget and personnel was limited. Despite the persistence of these challenges throughout his time in Japan, in the opening years of his service he had established the institutional stability of America's mission.

CHAPTER NINE

American Advisors, Americans' Problems

Tokyo – When John Bingham was named as minister to Japan, his skill as a diplomat was, as yet, untested. Now as the appointed senior representative of the American community in Japan, his constituency was much more diverse than his congressional district in eastern Ohio. And the political environment was perhaps even more complex. In addition to maintaining support from the administration and other interest groups back home, now he had to work with a government whose language and culture were not easy to understand. He also had to balance relationships with the other foreign diplomatic missions.

In handling the Taiwan expedition crisis, Bingham demonstrated a firm understanding of America's larger interests in the Pacific and a network in the region and back home that he could mobilize to protect American interests. He also showed a facility for working with both the Japanese government and the diplomatic community in Japan. On the indemnity and treaty issues, he set a course that American policy makers dealing with Japan for the next two decades would continue to follow. On policy matters his legal acumen and experience at political maneuvering enabled him to make a smooth transition to diplomacy. His adjustment to serving as nominal head of the wider American community in Japan required a longer apprenticeship.

Beyond their legations and consulates, by far the most visible component of each country's presence in Japan was its cadre of foreign experts, or *oyatoi gaikokujin*. In America's case, lack of Legation control over filling appointments to Japanese government positions had led to complaints about the quality of Americans filling these positions. Although there were superbly qualified individuals in this group, there were also misfits who had found their way to Japan and talked their way into a job. A passage from the contemporary press gives a flavor of the attitude of other nationalities regarding their American acquaintances.

> *Professors' in the schools of Tokei (Tokio) were graduates of the dry-goods counter, the forecastle, the camp, and the shambles, or belonged to that vast array of unclassified humanity that floats like waifs in every sea-port. Coming directly from the bar-room, the brothel, the gambling saloon, or the resort of boon companions, they brought the graces, the language, and the manners of these places into the schoolroom...[1]*

An American law passed in 1858 prevented overseas missions from lobbying foreign governments to hire American nationals. Bingham had lent his voice in opposition to this law, arguing that it put America at a disadvantage in competition with its European rivals. In June of 1874, Congress repealed the restrictive law, and Bingham was able to approach Meiji officials directly with recommendations for hiring specific individuals for designated positions.[2] Before that time, the Japanese government had made its own approaches to experts in the United States. In the addition to employing Horace

Capron for the Hokkaido project, these efforts resulted in the hiring of several prominent Americans whose service in Japan complemented Bingham's efforts. A common recruitment avenue was through the Japanese Legation in Washington, D.C., where Mori Arimori was the minister. Additionally, there were channels through missionaries such as Guido Verbeck and others connected to the American educational system. In contrast to his unofficial responsibility for the behavior and well-being of all American citizens living in or visiting Japan, the minister did have formal obligations under Japanese regulations for the *oyatoi*. These obligations, however, also had the benefit of opening many doors in the Japanese government to Bingham and his staff.

In addition to his relationship with Capron, Bingham's association with Dr. David Murray was critical during his earlier years in Japan. Murray's influence added content and depth to the Legation's influence with the Meiji government. A professor and renowned educator from Rutgers University, Murray was employed as education advisor to the Meiji government and had arrived in Japan several months before Bingham. Murray had contributed to Mori Arinori's *Education in America*, a tome Mori prepared in order to introduce America's educational system to Japan. Murray also had been a tutor to *Yoshida Kiyonari*, Mori's successor as Japan's minister to the United States. Hardly a "graduate of the dry-goods counter, the forecastle or the camp,"[3] Murray was a member of America's educational establishment elite. In speaking at a dinner honoring the New Jersey educator, Bingham used Murray's example to extoll personal and institutional cooperation between Japan and the United States.[4] And although his relationship with Murray was correct and cordial, such associations were not without irritants. Dr. Murray's wife wrote to a friend disparaging the Bingham's lack of social graces as very "Ohio."[5] Bingham's position as minister did not immunize him from eastern snobbery.

Two talented Americans who were employed with Horace Capron at the *Kaitakushi* were to play important parts later in Bingham's tour in Japan. The first, James Wasson, was a young man from Iowa who had attended West Point where he had been a classmate and close friend of President Grant's son, Frederick. Wasson was an outstanding student and the young Grant struggled academically, not unlike his father before him. In a letter to Horace Capron in Japan, dated January 26, 1872, Grant asked Capron to consider giving Wasson, who was a houseguest of the Grant's at the time, a position in the new Hokkaido organization.[6] In the letter Grant does showed appreciation for the importance of America's relations with Japan, and sees the *Kaitakushi* as playing a key role in building and enhancing that relationship. Bingham was to get to know the bright young soldier very well during the Taiwan crisis and then as his son-in-law. The second young man, Edwin Dun, like Bingham, was from Ohio. Dun had attended Miami University, in Ohio, and had become an expert in cattle raising, an enterprise central to Japanese plans for Hokkaido's development. Although he had no formal institutional responsibility for the *Kaitakushi*, Bingham was quite familiar with its personnel, given the organization's size and nature. During his years in Tokyo, Bingham became an important personal and professional mentor to Dun.

Another American already working for the Japanese government when Bingham arrived was even more "Ohio." Samuel MaGill Bryan had been born in Cadiz in 1847 and at only 14 years of age, had entered the Union army. In 1867, his local congressman, John Bingham, recommended Bryan for a clerkship with the Treasury Department in Washington, D.C. When the Iwakura Mission was in Washington, Bingham arranged to introduce the young Bryan to visiting Japanese officials. Bryan was offered a position in Japan. Relocating from Washington to Yokohama in February, 1873. Bryan assisted postal service negotiations between Japan and the United States and the result was a bilateral postal treaty signed in August. Bryan stayed on in Japan until 1883 at an annual salary of $6,000, a considerable sum, which made Bryan one of the wealthier residents of the Yokohama Bluff community. But rather than hometown camaraderie, the relationship between the hard-drinking Bryan and the proper and restrained Bingham was not good.[7] Bryan was an entrepreneur who made deals and lived fast. Bingham lived carefully and by the rules.

It is remarkable that in a very brief period of time, four young Ohioans from his region of Ohio, played an important role in Bingham's early interaction with Japan: missionary and interpreter David Thompson; soldier and educator L.L. Janes who had briefly worked at the Bingham law office in Cadiz just as Bingham was leaving for his first congressional term; executive and entrepreneur Samuel MaGill Bryan, and Eli T. Sheppard, whose advice from his post in Tianjin encouraged Bingham to consider an Asian posting.

Tsukiji, Yokohama - Many of the Bingham's closest relationships were with members of the missionary community. In 1858, the cross had followed the American flag with the conclusion by Townsend Harris of the Treaty of Amity and Commerce. Christianity remained proscribed by the Japanese government until 1873; and missions, particularly from Protestant denominations, had been setting up beachhead operations in the treaty ports since the late 1850s. The Civil War and lack of funding to support evangelical activities had slowed down the growth of American missionary activity during the 1860s; and by the time the Bingham family arrived in Japan, the American religious community in Yokohama, with an offshoot in Tsukiji in the capital, was well entrenched. The numbers were still small but were increasing; in 1873 alone, 29 new foreign missionaries arrived in Japan.[8] And although the new minister's duties assured contact with the wider American community, by volume, proximity and personal inclination, he was closest to the missionary community. The community's voluble participation in political issues only reinforced this relationship.

Even before 1873, when the Meiji government lifted the ban against Christian conversion efforts, in force since the early seventeenth century, the missionaries had become active in promoting and providing western-style education to an eager Japanese elite. In Nagasaki, where he first arrived in 1858, Guido Verbeck established a school where a number of the most important early Meiji leaders became pupils. This group included Okubo Toshimichi and Ito Hirobumi.[9] In the 1860s when anti-foreign violence in Japan was sometimes dramatic and deadly, Verbeck, as did many others, went armed when he was out in public.[10] In Tokyo by 1869, Verbeck was teaching at the *Kaisei* School which later became Tokyo Imperial University. For five years in the 1870s, Verbeck held a senior advisory position with the *Genro-in* or Chamber of Elders, an exclusive senior deliberative assembly where his counsel included translation and providing advice on education, conscription, and establishment of a western style medical system. During that period, Verbeck was a fellow resident in Tsukiji with the newly arrived minister. Verbeck's knowledge of the inner workings of the higher levels of the Meiji government was invaluable to Bingham. Less consequential but still important was Bingham's relationship with Reformed Church missionary James H. Ballagh who had important contacts among the leadership of missionary organizations back in Washington and New York.[11]

An incident that took place just a year after Bingham arrived in Japan highlighted how such relationships could shade into diplomatic episodes. The issue was the controversy over burials of two Japanese Christians in August and October, 1874, in Tokyo. Burial was not unheard of in Japan at the time, but cremation, which is almost universal today, was often mandated by the local government.[12] In this instance, explicitly Christian burial had been proscribed. The Tokyo court decided to take action against two Japanese Christians involved in the burials.[13] Thompson brought the issue to Bingham for assistance. Bingham advised Thompson to appear in person before the court.[14] This forthrightness helped to resolve the issue quietly. Veteran of countless standoffs in the House of Representatives and not a glutton for self-aggrandizement, Bingham understood well that private diplomacy at post without Washington's involvement was often more effective than public confrontation.

Hokkaido - When Alaska became American territory in 1867, the sea otter population came under renewed pressure from hunters and trappers. A single pelt was worth well over $100, worth more than $1,700 today, and sufficient to entice American trappers, already active along the Pacific coast from Oregon to Alaska, to Japan's northern reaches. At least four American trappers spent the winter of 1875 in a hut on the Hokkaido coast, huddled against the cold and warmed by dreams of wealth. According to the Treaty of 1858 they were in the wrong place, well outside the designated treaty port settlement areas. Characteristically Bingham searched for a legal remedy. While admitting the Japanese right to act against Americans beyond the designated treaty right areas, he suggested that the Meiji government issue a proclamation to make the policy on sea otter hunting more explicit. Fish suggested a more modest "semi-official notice of caution" be issued to the hunters.[15] The issue is peripheral but demonstrated Bingham's legalistic approach to problem solving.

Tokyo - This view of a legal dimension of right and wrong was the beginning of an important bond between Edwin Dun, an employee of the *Kaitakushi*, and the minister. From Chillicothe in the south-central part of the state, Dun's family were Democrats. But in 1875, those differences did not prevent Bingham from responding favorably when approached by Dun to marry him to his Japanese sweetheart. Dun's bride was from the family of a minor official. Intimate relations between Japanese and foreigners were not unusual but seldom legally or socially sanctioned. But Bingham appreciated that for Dun, whether in Japan or Ohio, the morally right way was also the legal way.[16] Bingham's assistance in legally marrying the couple established a lasting personal bond between the two men.

Bingham knew the legal text was clear when two Americans, including Civil War naval veteran and current USN Commander R.F.R. Lewis, were arrested in the summer of 1875 by local Japanese authorities in Hachioji. The two were charged with being outside the territory where foreigners were permitted to travel without a passport. Certainly, Hachijoji, which is now in the western suburbs of Tokyo, was beyond the area where foreign residents normally ventured. Still, it was, in fact, within the boundary of the foreign concession as stipulated in the Treaty which permitted foreigners to travel as much as twenty-five miles into the interior. Bingham immediately brought the case to the Ministry of Foreign Affairs. The Americans were released, the Japanese official punished, the men accepted the Japanese government's apology and thanked Minister Bingham. His measured approach calmed tempers in the foreign community.

Yokohama - Occasionally Consul General Van Buren asked for Minister Bingham's advice on handling specific cases. Yokohama could be a boisterous place, with its taverns for locals and visiting sailors on shore leave. The latter category of American citizens and not infrequently the former too, provided ample opportunity for legal intervention by the consulate. One example that illustrates the two men's often-strained relationship was Van Buren's request to Bingham for input on how to determine jurisdiction of an Italian sailor who was accused of murder while serving on an American vessel on the high seas. In a message to Secretary Fish, Bingham showed his frustration with Van Buren's inability to understand what lawyer Bingham saw as the rudiments of the law.[17] To Bingham such a case should be elementary, even if Van Buren had not formal legal training; American jurisdiction was obvious.

Tokyo – As minister, John Bingham's concern for Americans' welfare was not limited to working with the resident American community. As is still important to any embassy today, the Legation was tasked with escorting important visitors from back home. During his first full year in Japan, the freshly arrived minister planned the schedule and attended meetings at the Ministry of Foreign Affairs with Commodore George E. Belknap of the *Tuscarora*. The naval officer was visiting Japan to explore the best landing spot for submarine cables. Later in 1874 Bingham managed the schedule for a Professor Davidson, in Japan on a scientific mission to observe the transit of Venus.[18] Such activities may appear humdrum but they increased demands on time and limited resources. To be effective, the Legation had plenty of work to do, day in and day out.

As an Ohio Congressman, Bingham was familiar with the odd requests from constituents. Now he was fielding requests from across America. One request that remained among his personal papers when he passed away came from a dentist in Michigan. Apologizing for being unable to provide return Japanese stamps, the dentist asked Minister Bingham to approach the Emperor to give him an autograph for his collection.[19] Bingham took seriously his responsibility to serve and protect American citizens in Japan and to advance American interests.. With his tiny Legation staff, the Minister handled an assortment of matters, some weighty, some frivolous, but all important to the Americans involved.

In May of 1875, Horace Capron was leaving Japan after four years as head of the *Kaitakushi*. During his tenure, Capron had built the *Kaitakushi* into an effective organization that employed over thirty Americans. Japanese were already learning American farming techniques, and Capron had laid an important foundation for development of Hokkaido's dairy industry, which still flourishes today. Bingham and Capron made a round of courtesy calls, visiting Iwakura Tomomi and Okubo Toshimichi, two of the most powerful figures in the Meiji government. Capron shared Bingham's view that America should revise her unequal treaty with Japan, and the visits were an opportunity for both sides to share warm reminiscences. Capron and his management of the *Kaitakushi* had been a target of derision in the local British press but this only reinforced his rapport with the minister.[20]

Less than two years into his stay in Japan, Bingham had built ties of mutual understanding that reinforced his effectiveness in his role as a bridge between the two nations. Showing firmness on the Taiwan adventure, encouraging the Japanese government to hire skilled Americans, and strengthening ties with Americans who were doing important work in Japan, he set a solid foundation for his effectiveness as a diplomat. Just as importantly, he had learned to admire what Japan was accomplishing, and Japanese leaders had come to appreciate the American minister for his diligence and discretion.[21]

CHAPTER TEN
Transition, Mentors and Unrest in Japan

Washington, Kagoshima - Bingham had settled into his role as minister but news reaching Tokyo was mixed. Reports from Philadelphia were exciting as America celebrated the centennial of its Declaration of Independence from Britain. Japan was well represented as the United States held its first official world's fair. Political developments were less encouraging. Grant's term was coming to an end and the ability of Bingham's Republican Party to hold onto the White House was in doubt. Uncertainty would mean a scramble for positions among Bingham's younger associates. In Japan, there were stirrings of subversive anti-Meiji activity in Kyushu, the southernmost of Japan's four main islands.

Philadelphia – Japanese participation in the 1876 Philadelphia Centennial Exposition had an enormous and positive impact on the image of Japan among the American public. Open from May 10 to November 10, the Exposition boasted two hundred buildings constructed for the fair. Most impressive was Machinery Hall which housed eight thousand operating machines. Many Americans saw bananas, popcorn, and catsup for the first time when they visited Philadelphia. Alexander Graham Bell exhibited his new invention, the telephone, and in the Horticultural Hall the miracle Asian plant, *kudzu*, was introduced and touted as easy to grow, easy to maintain, and perfect for creating excellent shade.[1] The fair attracted 37 national participants and almost ten million visitors. No longer the "double-bolted" land Melville described two decades earlier, Japanese artistic sensitivities had been seeping into western art in the years before the Philadelphia fair. Two years before the fair's opening, Bingham had strongly urged the Japanese to participate. They were eager to do so and to make the most of the opportunity. After 1876, the trickle of American interest in Japan became a flood. And the deluge was not limited to paintings and ceramics but extended to architecture and craftsmanship more broadly.

The fair was a media sensation, covered extensively by national magazines including the *Atlantic Monthly* and *Harper's Magazine*, which set elite cultural trends of the times. The attention from mass circulation daily newspapers was equally energetic. Japan, bringing in a crew of craftsmen, artists and builders, created a pavilion, a bazaar and a garden which impressed visitors and readers alike. Descriptions of the Japanese exhibit from the *Atlantic Monthly's* July 1876 edition recall the impact of the Japanese displays.

> *The Japanese seem to possess the secret which the modern pre-Raphaelites have striven for without success, the union of detail and effect; ...An enumeration of even the most striking objects in the Japanese department would be the driest of catalogues; description can give no idea of them; wherever you look, the eye is delighted and contented...*

Japanese Pavilion – Collection of National Gallery of Art.

THE JAPANESE DWELLING.

After the Japanese collection, everything looks in a measure commonplace, almost vulgar. The English embroidery and china in imitation of their models are either pitiably weak or like feverish fancies, quite disordered and unnatural.

The whole nearer East looks dim and rough after the splendor and sheen of Japan. China strikes one as elaborately ugly and grotesque...[2]

The media mood was clear. Japan was a hit in Philadelphia. In the next decades, the fascination with Japanese art and culture would continue to grow and flourish. The positive mood even reached the Department of State. Not one for rhetorical flourishes, Hamilton Fish wrote to Bingham to praise the Japanese exhibit at the fair.[3]

The Philadelphia Exhibition did not simply provide Japan with an opportunity to rouse interest in Japanese aesthetics. In seminars held as part of the program, Japan presented her advancements in other fields to audiences of experts. For example, Japan participated in the International Conference on Education. During the conference, Dr. David Murray, education advisor to the Meiji government, gave educators, gathered from a dozen countries and two dozen American states, a detailed account of Japan's progress in instituting modern educational systems and reforms.

The exhibition also allowed Japanese visitors to learn more about what American products Japan might want. The British had built Japan's first railroad connecting Yokohama to Tokyo in 1872. In early 1877, Bingham and his interpreter Thompson, joined the diplomatic corps on a visit to Kyoto. The diplomats were there to attend the ceremony in which the Emperor Meiji celebrated the opening of the Hyogo to Kyoto rail line. The only speaking part for a foreign dignitary went to Sir Harry Parkes. Always jealous of Parkes and bolstered by reports from Philadelphia, Bingham was determined to break British dominance of Japan's rail market. Baldwin Locomotive Works, based in Philadelphia, had had an impressive presence at the fair, that company's first step towards Japan market success, a success that Bingham was able to foster. Also on exhibit in Philadelphia had been the derrick from the Drake Well in Titusville, Pennsylvania, the first American oil well. America had become a force to reckon with in the kerosene production and export business. Kerosene was to become America's main export to Japan.

Montana Territory - Just as America was celebrating the centennial of the Declaration of Independence, a tragedy befell a young man who is perhaps the best remembered of all those whose careers were launched by Bingham. As visitors were streaming into the Philadelphia Exposition and as a lopsided baseball game was played by Americans at the cricket grounds in Yokohama, the *Helena Herald* was first to report the killings in the battle of the Little Big Horn. Twenty years earlier, Bingham had nominated George Armstrong Custer for admission to the Military Academy at West Point. With his death, the brash young soldier soon became an American archetype, far outstripping his congressional sponsor in fame and in more recent years, notoriety. Custer had made his last stand.

The Indians poured in a murderous fire from all directions, and the greatest portion fought on horseback. General Custar (sic), his two brothers, nephew and brother-in- law were all killed, and not one of his detachment escaped. Two hundred and seven   men were buried in one place, and the number of killed is estimated at three hundred, with ouly (sic) thirty-one wounded.[4]

Today, Americans, whose interest in history often focusses on military figures, are still more likely to read about Bingham as the congressman who recommended Custer to West Point than to learn about his contributions as a legislator and diplomat.

Ohio - John Bingham recognized that the presidential election of 1876 would be a difficult one for his Republican Party. Corruption scandals had wounded the Grant Administration and the national mood of the electorate was balking at the challenges of Reconstruction. In June, the party's selection of Rutherford B. Hayes to lead the ticket was an encouraging development. Bingham knew Hayes well. When the 39th Congress voted to approve the 14th amendment in June of 1868, freshman Representative Rutherford B. Hayes voted to approve.[5] He also voted for the impeachment of Andrew Johnson. Elected governor of Ohio by a thin margin the next year, Hayes continued to support the Republican Party's Reconstruction agenda. On the broad range of issues facing post-Civil War Ohio, Hayes and Bingham held compatible views. After extensive campaigning together during September 1870, an election where both retained their seats, Bingham lauded not his own but "our success" in his 16th District.[6] The tone of their correspondence at the time and in the years after, showed that the two men had a personal bond as well as mutual professional respect. In the lead-up to the November general election, Hayes and Bingham exchanged letters. Replying to Bingham's August 11 letter, Hayes expressed genuine concern that the prospects of a Republican victory in November were in doubt.[7]

Although Hayes won a closely-contested Republican nomination in the summer, neither he nor his Democratic opponent, Samuel Tilden, was able to take a majority in the Electoral College. As the election outcome hung in the balance for weeks, once again, as he had done as consul in Tientsin, Sheppard was able to pass along inside information to his mentor, Bingham. After leaving his American diplomatic post in China in the fall, Sheppard was back in the United States. Visiting Ohio in December while the Electoral College was still deadlocked, Sheppard met with Hayes who reassured Sheppard that if confirmed the victor by the Electoral College, he had every intention of keeping Bingham as minister in Tokyo. Sheppard wrote to Bingham that Hayes had said "He would no more think of having you removed than if you were his father."[8] In a letter less than two weeks earlier, Sheppard had described the dire mood in the United States where rifle clubs in the South and surrounding Washington, D.C., threatened free democracy and had created a political "volcano."[9]

Tokyo – The electoral impasse was resolved by the Compromise of 1877, an agreement that most historians mark as the end of Reconstruction. Rutherford B. Hayes became president and the remaining federal troops were removed from formerly Confederate states. The United States continued as a unified nation, but there would no longer be a federal government effort to enforce the social gains of Reconstruction. Bingham's dreams for racial progress in America were thwarted, but his hopes to advance policy aims in Japan were still very much alive. He was relieved by Hayes' victory and pleased to stay as America's minister to the Meiji government. Since late January, the government had been under increasing threat of an armed insurrection by forces gathering on the southern island of Kyushu.

For Bingham, the tension caused by the uncertainty of the electoral results and the difficulty in getting the latest information brought additional irritations. For the far away minister who paid almost as much attention to his pocketbook as to politics, receiving timely reports from back home was expensive. Writing from Cadiz, friend David Cunningham informed Bingham that an earlier telegram he had sent about election results had cost $24.80 in gold, $27.28 in currency which Cunningham said he would deduct from Bingham's Cadiz bank account.[10]

From the beginning of his assignment in Japan, Bingham worked closely with several young Americans who went on to make significant contributions to the Japanese bilateral diplomatic relationship. The reason Sheppard was back in the States and was able to report back to Bingham in Tokyo was because he was taking leave with his family before assuming an important position with the Japanese government. Bingham had helped arrange for Sheppard to become legal advisor, replacing the brilliant and colorful Erastus Peshine Smith.[11]

Bingham's support of Sheppard's move to the Japanese government position was not without drama. He was well aware that nurturing the American relationship with Japan required cultivating younger Americans of good character who were committed to that relationship. And the uncertainty in American politics made it all the more critical to have sympathetic Americans in positions of influence in both the Japanese and American governments. In 1876, the third year of Minister Bingham's tour in Japan, three of these aspirants approached their mentor separately for help in getting a position as a legal advisor to the Ministry of Foreign Affairs.

In January, Eli T. Sheppard had written to his fellow Ohioan and mentor in Tokyo, asking for assistance in obtaining a position on the Law Faculty of Japan's Imperial University, a position in which he would also serve as a legal advisor to the Japanese government.[12] Sheppard had a young family. and his position at the consulate in Tientsin was unclear given the uncertain prospects in the fall election. Japanese government jobs paid well and from his correspondence with Bingham when Bingham was being considered for the Tokyo slot, Sheppard made it clear that he felt Tokyo would be a pleasant assignment.

In April, Henry Denison wrote to Bingham, asking to be considered for the appointment to the legal advisor position. Denison, who along with his wife had played such major parts in the Van Buren - Bingham melodrama, had left his position as legal staff at the Consulate General of Yokohama at the end of 1875. Denison wanted to continue working in Japan and had found employment in Yokohama as a private attorney. In applying for the Ministry of Foreign Affairs position, Denison was confident the minister had a positive opinion of his character and competence. But in approaching Bingham, he suspected another Bingham protégé might have aspirations for the appointment. Denison wrote the minister that he understood Bingham's deputy at the Legation, Durham Stevens, might also be interested. Though he said he did not want to stand in Stevens' way, Denison did add that he wanted Bingham to be aware of his interest.[13] Denison did not realize that Sheppard, writing from Tientsin, had already put in his request.

Solicitation for the job on behalf of Durham Stevens arrived from Stevens' father, Bingham's longtime friend and a key connection to the Washington political scene. Stevens was working in Washington at the time at the Department of the Interior, Bureau of Indian Affairs.[14] Apologizing for being a poor correspondent, Stevens, both updated Bingham on Ohio politics and urged appointment of his son to the legal position. Writing from Washington Stevens described the difficult position the Republican Party was facing in Ohio with the upcoming presidential election. A possible change in administrations might mean that both his job in Washington and his son's position in Japan were in jeopardy.

Bingham carefully considered the advantages and drawbacks of each of these three candidates. Sheppard was an established family man with several children and a wife who was close to Bingham's Cadiz relatives. These considerations gave Bingham personal as well as professional reasons to push the Sheppard appointment with his Japanese government contacts. Another consideration was that at the Legation, Bingham had come to depend on Legation Secretary Stevens and knew there would be a risk if Stevens were to leave. Washington could control the appointment for a successor and might saddle the

Legation with a less competent officer. If he were able to maintain his position as minister, Bingham wanted to retain Stevens as a reliable right hand partner. Denison, though capable, was young and had no political or personal connections back in Ohio. Thus on Bingham's recommendation, Sheppard joined the law faculty and became legal advisor to the Japanese government.

Kagoshima - In Japan, just weeks earlier than America's controversial transfer of power, rebellion against central Meiji authority broke into open violence. The Satsuma Rebellion was the last great military challenge to the new Japanese order. Called the Southwest War in Japanese sources, the rebellion was led by Saigo Takamori, whose planned expedition to Korea had been squashed by the returning Iwakura Mission leaders in 1873. Saigo had returned to his native Kyushu and had organized military style schools in the Kagoshima area. When fighting started between Saigo's forces and the Imperial Army, it was not clear that the Meiji government would prevail. "And if it succeeded," wrote respected scholar Donald Keene, "the entire political configuration of Japan would undoubtedly have changed."[15] These were momentous months in both countries.

Bingham recognized the threat posed by the southern samurai insurrection. In a series of messages addressed to Secretary Fish from February through April 1877, Bingham outlined the events taking place in Kyushu during the Satsuma uprising. In the last of these messages, Bingham informed the Secretary that the Imperial troops had captured Kumamoto Castle, the rebels' stronghold. It was a major victory for the central government. Bingham, in a familiar argument, emphasized that high taxes were a major contributor to the rebels' anger. For Bingham, the Satsuma uprising provided yet another clear demonstration that the unequal treaties must be revised. Bingham knew Fish would be out of office and would not receive the last of these messages. But he hoped to reach the new secretary's inbox. [16]

Washington, D.C. The Compromise of 1877 suspended any progress on Bingham's dreams for the nurturing of a more racially just society back home. But with Hayes in the White House, he was more optimistic on the chances to move forward on bilateral trade issues with Japan. Relieved by the final news of Hayes' win; he was thrilled by the lineup of leaders Hayes brought in to manage America's foreign affairs. Hayes' choice for secretary of state, William Evarts, knew Bingham well. Before entering politics, Evarts had been a skilled litigator, and later was elected to the Senate from New York. He had faced off against Bingham as Attorney General and chief counsel for President Andrew Johnson's defense in the impeachment trial. Despite being on opposing sides in the Johnson trial, Evarts and Bingham were not political antagonists.

Evarts' selection as secretary of state was not surprising. He had been a member of the electoral commission that worked to resolve the Hayes-Tilden election. Evart's father, Jeremiah Evarts, was a noted religious writer and publisher of a journal, *The Panoplist,* which was absorbed by *The Missionary Herald* in 1820. The elder Evarts was retained as editor. He also acted as Treasurer of the Board of Commissioners for Foreign Missions, an organization deeply involved with the American missionary community in Meiji Japan. [17] The backgrounds and experiences of the minister to Japan and the secretary of state overlapped. Their political and personal networks reinforced each other.

For regular communications with the State Department there

was an added personal contact that promised greater efficiency than during Hamilton Fish's term. Now, Frederick William Seward, son of wartime secretary of state, who had done so much to solidify American interests in the Pacific, became assistant secretary of state. In June, Seward wrote to Bingham, thanking him for his kind words on his appointment. "Such words from my father's old friends…" Seward wrote, "constitute one of my chief pleasures in returning to my old post."[18] Seward had served before as assistant secretary during his father's tenure as secretary in the Lincoln and Johnson cabinets. By May, Eli Sheppard had returned to Tokyo to take up employment as legal advisor to the Japanese government. The network Bingham had helped build in Tokyo, complemented by his close associations with key leaders in Washington, was now moving into place.

Tokyo - The people in John Bingham's world were on the move. In September, Consul General Van Buren left Yokohama for a six-month home leave. By December, the Chinese had arrived in Tokyo with a full diplomatic complement, the second Asian country to establish a mission. The Koreans had arrived in June of the previous year after Japan concluded the Treaty of *Kanghwa (Ganghwa)* with the Korean kingdom. The outlines of the new diplomatic arrangements in northeast Asia now had concrete expression in the Japanese capital.

The Bingham's family life was also in transition. Daughter Marie and the ambitious Major Wasson were married the same month as the opening of the Philadelphia Centennial Exposition. Then in January of 1877, the newlywed couple left Japan for a new life in America. After a brief stay in Washington, Major Wasson and Marie relocated to San Antonio, Texas.[19] On August 1, 1877, John and Amanda Bingham's grandson, Robert Bingham Wasson, was born.

CHAPTER ELEVEN

Policy Engagement with the Hayes Administration

Tokyo - With Hamilton Fish in retirement, his friend Hayes in the White House and the rebellion in Kyushu as an object lesson, Bingham renewed his crusade for treaty revision. In a message to Secretary Evarts, Bingham described Japan's progress and expressed his confidence in its future in a way that sums up his view of America's historical destiny:

> *It is but the truth of history to say that since his accession to the throne, in 1868, this young Emperor, now but twenty-eight years of age, and representing the oldest continuous dynasty on earth....has...been constantly mindful of the rights of his people, and, within his short reign of twelve years abolished the feudal system, emancipated four-fifths of his subjects from feudal vassalage, and made them possessors of the soil; disarmed a feudal soldiery number probable [sic] 600,000 men trained to arms; reorganized the order of society; established and equipped an army 40,000 strong, and also a navy equal in number and appointments to our own; assured the freedom of conscience;*

introduced the press, the telegraph, the railway, steam
navigation, a general postal and savings system, and,
above all, ordained a free system of compulsory education
for the instruction of all the children of the empire, thereby
in effect declaring the equality of all before the law, and
the right of each to the equal protection of the law.[1]

Bingham recognized that abrogation of extraterritorial rights for American citizens would not be acceptable in Washington but that separate talks on revision of the tariff rules might be possible. With Hayes settled in office and with the prospect of the President's annual address at the end of the year looming, Bingham renewed his campaign to address the treaty issue. Becoming somewhat more formal than in his more personal letters to Hayes during earlier Ohio campaigns, Bingham wrote directly to the president in a letter dated September 8, 1877.[2] Complementing the president and Secretary of State Evarts for their public commitment to promote America's foreign commerce, Bingham reminded President Hayes, and other staff whom he knew would also read the message, that he had been championing revision of America's unequal treaty with Japan since he first took up his ministerial duties. Citing the messages that he had received from Evarts indicating the State Department's willingness to move ahead on revision, Bingham continued to provide references and justifications. [3]

Referring to messages sent to the Department beginning in 1874, Bingham described attempts by Europeans, especially the British, to muzzle him on the treaty issue. Not simply criticizing the Europeans, a popular political stance, he also listed the benefits that could be realized if the treaties were to be revised. American traders could increase their business, government import tariff collection would increase, and American influence within the foreign community in Japan would grow. In related communications, Evarts had requested reports from post about how the Legation might improve business between Japan and America. Bingham conveyed suggestions from meetings he had with Vice Foreign Minister Terashima and an American businessman. In one message he launched into a detailed description of the poor quality of British textiles which he wrote, are "loaded with terra alba and starch to give appearance and weight, but being washed prove to be the flimsiest material known to the trade."[4] For Bingham, treaty revision would unleash practical, concrete successes for American traders.

Bingham continued to argue that an important cause of the Satsuma Rebellion was Japan's inability under the unequal treaties to collect sufficient revenue. Among their grievances against the government, the rebels had cited failure to rid Japan of the hated treaties. Bingham argued that since the Japanese government was prohibited by the treaties from collecting higher customs duties, there was no alternative but to rely on onerous agricultural taxes. This, in turn, fueled social unrest. As the rebellion was being put down, Bingham wrote Evarts that he had "unofficially and informally" told his Japanese interlocutors that the best policy after victory over the rebels would be to "season justice with mercy."[5] In a second letter later that year, providing an overview of the situation, Bingham blamed the crushing tax burden resulting from the low tariffs fixed by the treaty powers as a cause of the Satsuma Rebellion.[6]

Bingham was not alone in advocating a separate agreement that would allow Japan more control over custom duties while keeping other provisions of the unequal treaties in force. In a meeting between Secretary Fish and Japanese Minister to Washington Yoshida Kiyonari in 1876, the two governments explored addressing tariff provisions alone.[7] In his diary, British diplomat Ernest Satow, reported a conversation in Europe in April 1876, when discussions within the British government covered key provisions of the treaty and the question of whether these selected provisions should be revised. Although the discussion ended with an agreement that revision was premature, the fact that such conversations were underway was significant.[8]

Unqualified support for the unequal treaties in the expatriate community in Japan and in the English language press was also eroding. Quoting figures from a *New York Times* article, the *Daily Japan Herald* on July 28, 1877, provided data showing that only 4% of Japan's imports came from the United States. The figure for the United Kingdom was 62%.[9] Allowing Japan to set protective duties was a threat to British commercial interests but of marginal concern to Americans. To Bingham, treaty revision could be a useful tool with which to begin to chip away at British market dominance. Bingham's efforts were to result in an agreement for the United States and Japan to begin negotiations on the treaty issue.

Washington, D.C. – Once underway, the atmosphere surrounding the early Japanese and American talks on treaty revision was optimistic. A formula that would allow Japan to set its own customs duties while leaving much of the extraterritorial legal structure in place seemed like a timely and practical solution. Once negotiations began in Washington, it did not take Minister Yoshida and Secretary Evarts long to reach agreement.

On July 25, 1878, they fixed their signatures and seals on an

John Bingham's counterpart and friend, Yoshida Kiyonari, Japanese Minister to Washington, 1874-1882. Reprint in author's private collection.

agreed Convention. In Article I of the Convention, the United States recognized that Japan had the right to set customs duties and to regulate foreign commerce. Additional articles clarified other duty provisions and gave Japan authority to regulate Japanese coastal trade.[10]

Article X, the final article, however, was problematic. Under its provisions, the parties agreed that the entire Convention would not go into effect until all the other treaty powers had concurred. Initially, details of the new agreement remained tightly held, but when word got out, American journalist Edward House, proprietor, *Tokio Times*, was furious.[11] House called Japan's inclusion of Article X a major diplomatic mistake that rendered the agreement meaningless.[12] Bingham's immediate reaction was to suggest to Evarts that the agreement be modified to remove Article X. The parties then would allow the Convention to take effect upon exchange of ratifications. As Bingham had anticipated, the British and Germans strongly attacked the Convention and its brazen American deviation from the Cooperative Policy.

The Convention of 1878 was approved by the Senate on December 18, 1878, signed by President Hayes on January 20, 1879, ratified by Japan on February 7 and entered into force on April 8, 1879. But it entered into force only on paper. Japan had opened similar negotiations with other treaty powers and was naively hopeful that signing the agreement with the United States would facilitate finalizing agreements with the other treaty powers. It did not.[13] Although House may have been correct in calling the agreement a diplomatic disaster for Japan, it did have the positive effect of advancing the treaty revision process. For all parties, revision was now on the table. The form revision would take and the speed at which it might go forward were still uncertain. But the fissures among the treaty powers were unmistakable. And any dissent within America's often quixotic foreign policy making process was now resolved. Both the American administration and Congress were on the record for revision. Payson Treat, writing a century ago, said that the Convention of 1878 was "merely a friendly gesture on the part of the United States to keep alive the issue of revision."[14] While disappointed that the negotiations had not helped the United States jettison the vestiges of the Cooperative Policy, the effort did signal to the Japanese that America was willing to move forward. And, of course, Hayes and Evarts had taken a move that was popular with elements of America's political elite and with the missionary and education community in the heartland. Politically, American policymakers had not failed. Rather, Washington politicians were able to complain that American efforts to bring justice and fairness to the relationship with Japan had been thwarted by European, particularly British, commercial rapacity.

On another issue, Bingham was pleased for continued support back home for returning the Shimonoseki Indemnity, but the pace of progress remained slow. Congress had long wanted to resolve the issue. In 1876, the Senate had passed a bill to return the indemnity to Japan. In the House, the issue died in committee. In 1877, bills were brought forward in both houses, but action was taken on neither. Bingham was encouraged that Japan and the indemnity issue remained a topic of policy discussion. He also hoped that with the improvement in the American economy and the government's fiscal condition, Congress might soon have the resources to act accordingly.

Tokyo – The Legation's credibility among Washington officials was reinforced by the volume and quality of reporting from Japan. Under Bingham's management, the American mission in Japan had enjoyed a banner year in 1876. Such reporting could be particularly important in a year of political transition. Then as now, the reputation of the overseas mission and its individual officers was closely related to the quality of information provided to the Department. With fellow Cadizian and borrowed missionary David Thompson firmly established as interpreter, Bingham's Legation cranked out lengthy reports on a number of developments including Japan's new banking laws, copyright law, and mining and shipping regulations. Worried that the Thompson position was up for deletion by parsimonious State Department budget cutters, Bingham used the opportunity of transmitting these reports to emphasize the value of the mission's reporting. Under Bingham's management, the volume and quality of the Legation's reporting was impressive and far exceeded that of his predecessors.

CHAPTER TWELVE

Bingham Family Takes Home Leave

Tsukiji – John and Amanda Bingham had become accustomed to life in Tokyo but missed friends and family back home. Since leaving for Japan five years earlier, they had not seen their daughter Lucy, and her young family in Pittsburgh. And now they wanted to see daughter Marie, and their new grandson in Texas. Always anxious about his finances, John Bingham needed to check on his bank accounts and property in Ohio. Amanda Bingham wanted to see her family and friends in Cadiz. John also wanted to renew professional contacts and use his personal network to advance his policy goals with Japan. His position as minister was secure until the next presidential election in 1880. And in Durham Stevens he had a reliable deputy to manage the Legation in his absence. It was time to take home leave.

While planning his home leave, sad personal news reached the Binghams in Tokyo. Tragically, the expectation of a pleasant family reunion was shattered. Daughter Lucy in Pittsburgh had died suddenly of a heart attack in September. The sermon at Tokyo Union Church on Sunday, October 6, honoring Lucy's life was scant comfort to the Bingham family.[1] With heavy hearts, John and Amanda, with daughter Emma, left Yokohama for San Francisco and home on the

City of Tokio the last week of October, 1878.

Daughter Marie's letters from Texas, where her husband was stationed were also worrying. Marie's letters to her dear "papa" had become melodramatic and betrayed a deep homesickness and dissatisfaction with her life in Texas. The young couple's son, Robert, was just a toddler, but Marie was finding that the life of an Army wife was a forlorn and often lonely existence. She decided to return to Japan with her son and parents rather than stay with her husband. Texas and Tokyo were very different types of frontier. And while John and Amanda hoped the couple could soon be united, Marie had become aware of Major Wasson's crippling character weaknesses.

Washington, D.C. – Politics offered little solace. The mid-term elections occurring as Bingham traveled home added to the darkness. As a result, the 46th Congress that was seated in March, 1879, saw Bingham's Republican Party in the minority with 132 seats to the Democrats 141 and 13 for the Greenback Party. In the Senate too, the Democrats won a firm majority. In Bingham's home state of Ohio, the Republicans lost three seats to the Democrats and the Senate seat went from a Republican to a Democrat, George Pendleton.

Bingham had a list of reasons he needed to visit Washington and the changes there meant his personal involvement was all the more important. He knew President Hayes well and believed a personal appeal on both resolution of the Shimonoseki Indemnity and the treaty revision issues would be helpful. Hayes' support and that of his allies on Capitol Hill was now vital, since any final resolution of both issues was in the hands of Congress. Aware that anti-Chinese immigration legislation was looming in Congress, Bingham also wanted to lobby allies and explain the potential negative impact of anti-Asian sentiment on American policy in East Asia. Meeting with officials in the State Department and with members of the House Appropriations Committee, he sought to secure and even increase the mission's funding and hoped to add an additional American officer to his staff.

Bingham also suspected that with Van Buren back in Washington on his own home leave, there might be some cleaning up to do. He had picked up rumors that others were angling for his ministerial spot. The year before, Bingham had recommended a young naval officer, Lt. J. Barton, to his friend President Hayes for an assignment back in Washington.[2] Barton had proven useful to Bingham as a source of gossip in the nation's capital and had written to reassure Bingham that he was secure in his position. There was no possibility, Barton said, that Van Buren would replace him as minister.[3] In the meantime, former President Grant had left Philadelphia on the 17th and was on his way to Great Britain to begin a trip around the world.[4] The trip was to conclude with a visit to Japan and Bingham wanted to help shape the schedule to make sure Grant's visit maximized the opportunities to further improve America's relationship with Japan.

In addition to American officials, Bingham was also eager to meet with his Japanese counterpart, Yoshida Kiyonari, to get his assessment of the bilateral relationship and Yoshida's prospects for his own career. Much younger and more gregarious than his American counterpart, Yoshida kept up a congenial personal correspondence with Bingham. never failing to mention important family events in their respective lives. He had been particularly excited to share the news of his daughter's birth in Washington, knowing how Bingham prized his daughters. Personal and business motivations were never separate for diplomats living with their families in foreign countries.[5] Yoshida was close to Okubo Toshimichi, whose assassination earlier that year had been the most important political event in Japan in 1878. Okubo was "undoubtedly the most powerful man in the government, responsible only to the emperor."[6] and Bingham knew that with Okubo gone, personnel changes would be likely. Yoshida's letter had also alerted Bingham to proposed plans for former President Grant's world tour and preparations for his upcoming visit to Japan.

Okubo's death had affected Bingham greatly. His messages to Evarts on the occasion of the assassination took on a different and darker tone from that of most of his reports. Bingham's formal communications with Washington were sometimes long-winded, often legalistic and rarely emotional. If he did refer to his personal beliefs, Bingham adhered to the standard, dominant civic Protestant world view of his generation: there is a Maker, that Maker has a purpose and it is America's national destiny to help fulfill that purpose. In a message to Evarts, Bingham, prosecutor of Lincoln's assassins, wrote that Okubo had received a letter foretelling his death. It was reminiscent of the Selby letter presented as evidence at the Lincoln assassins' conspiracy trial. The similarity of these two letters warning of conspiracy, and the fatalistic response from both Lincoln and Okubo when they received these letters, was haunting to Bingham.[7]

Additionally, Bingham had earlier told Evarts that the Emperor had sent a letter directly to Okubo, even after he knew the important Meiji leader had been killed. That the Emperor would explicitly address a message to a deceased person as if that person were still alive struck Bingham as a glimpse into the Japanese potential for belief in an afterlife, a belief Bingham held. Bingham wrote "There is something very impressive in the simple faith of this people, that their dead still live."[8] Bingham's response to these two letters to Okubo and his willingness to share these thoughts offered a rare peek into Bingham's spiritual makeup. Normally stoic and rational, even when speaking of matters of faith, the tone of these messages presented a veiled counterpoint. Certainly, by the time that he had arrived in Washington, Bingham was confident of one thing and that was that the assassination would not likely produce political chaos in Japan. The reformers there would retain control. As for Yoshida, he was to remain as minister in Washington and would be on hand to greet and escort President Grant when he arrived in Japan the following year.

At dinner with old Ohio friend President Hayes at the White House, both men could air their hopes and fears. In Japan, the tone of political discourse with the western countries was becoming more assertive. In America, the mood was turning from a focus on the needs of redressing the evils of slavery toward reconciliation of northern and southern white elites.[9] Changes in both societies were consequential and inexorable. The president and minister had much to talk about.

CHAPTER THIRTEEN
Grant's Visit to Japan

Nagasaki, Kobe, Tokyo - Just weeks after returning from home leave, John Bingham prepared to welcome former president Grant for a visit that was to feature elaborate ceremony and political consequence. Diplomatic protocol, then as now, required that the top ranked diplomats of both the host and visiting nations be on hand for arrival of an official visitor of Grant's stature. Japanese Minister Yoshida had also just returned to Japan and traveled with the American minister to greet Grant when he landed in Japan. Grant and his entourage landed on Japanese soil at Nagasaki on June 21, 1879, having left *Chefoo* (Yentai), China three days earlier. Bingham had been preparing for the visit since first alerted by a message from Yoshida two years earlier.[1]

Grant's two-month long visit is still acknowledged today as one of the highest peaks of good feeling between the two nations. Japanese leaders knew Grant well and were hoping to use the visit to leverage American willingness to engage on treaty revision and to move forward on resolving the Shimonoseki Indemnity. Other factors were animating positive feelings toward America. Many high officials had children studying in American universities. And unlike some other foreign countries, the Americans seemed serious about having no territorial designs in northeast Asia.

More than two years earlier, Grant had left for a trip that had taken him to Europe, the Holy Land, through the Suez Canal to India, Southeast Asia and on to China. Japan was the last stop. The Dutch had maintained a small trading outpost on *Dejima*, a tiny man-made island in Nagasaki's harbor, throughout the Tokugawa Shogunate's closed "doubled bolted" years. For more than two centuries, Dejima was the only official access point for western contact and provided Japan a narrow but important window on the West. The Chinese population in Nagasaki was much larger than the few westerners who resided there and the volume of trade with China, still small, dwarfed the trade through the Dutch. Grant and his party arrived in Nagasaki to a welcome that was warm and enthusiastic. One guest's sated description of the welcoming banquet prepared for the Americans: "The dinner came to an end after a struggle of six to seven hours..." described Japanese hospitality so overwhelming as to be almost brutal.[2] During their stay in Nagasaki, General and Mrs. Grant both planted commemorative trees, the most prominent Americans to participate in a Japanese tradition that dated at least to the Heian Period, a millennium earlier in Japan's storied past.

As the *U.S.S. Richmond* left Nagasaki and sailed through the Shimonoseki Straits into the Inland Sea, on board were former president Ulysses S. Grant, Minister John Bingham and Minister Yoshida Kiyonari. The three shared political perspectives and personal connections. As president, Grant had shown an interest in Japan and welcomed the Iwakura Mission to the White House in 1872.. Also on board the *Richmond* was Mrs. Grant and Grant's son, Frederick, who was accompanying his father on the round the world tour. Frederick Grant was a close friend of Bingham's son-in-law, James Wasson, now serving as army paymaster in Texas while his wife Marie and their son, Robert were living in Tokyo. As they sat on the deck and enjoyed the coastal scenery, all three men shared a vision of a Japan free from the restraints and humiliation of the unequal treaties, a Japan that was independent and a growing partner in trade

Proceeding from Nagasaki, Grant's party planned to go ashore at Hyogo (Kobe) and then tour Japan's ancient capital of Kyoto. But just months before Grant's arrival, an unwelcome guest had appeared in Japan, cholera. After a scare in the fall of 1877, when the dreaded disease did not appear in force, it had finally entered Japan in the spring of 1879 with great impact. Japan had instituted quarantine restrictions to cope with diseases coming into the country from overseas. However, the western powers' willingness to observe these regulations had become a major source of controversy among the treaty powers. It was a fight which had broader implications for extraterritoriality in general.

For Grant's group, the immediate consequence of the cholera scare was the forced cancellation of shore visits in the Kansai region. Hyogo Consul Julius Stahel was able to pay a call on the former president and his entourage aboard the *Richmond*. But, as guests of the Emperor and out of respect for the Japanese quarantine, the American visitors did not go ashore. One compensation, perhaps, was that since steaming directly to Yokohama would have put the Americans awkwardly ahead of schedule, they sailed at a more leisurely speed during daylight hours and anchored during the night. This slower progression provided an excellent opportunity to enjoy the picturesque scenery along Japan's Inland Sea.

On July 3, as scheduled, Grant and his entourage arrived at Yokohama, met there by the Meiji government's most senior official, Iwakura Tomomi, Consul General Thomas Van Buren, and other dignitaries After a train ride from Yokohama to Shimbashi, the group was escorted to the *Enryokan*, a compound that had been a summer palace during the Shogunate and which served as a guest house for foreign dignitaries. More formal activities were to follow ex-President Grant's official ceremonial call upon the Emperor, scheduled propitiously and intentionally for July 4.

At one-thirty on American Independence Day, Bingham arrived at the Enryokan to escort Grant and his party to their audience with His Imperial Majesty. John Russell Young, a journalist who was invited along on the world tour and who had become quite close to Grant during their two years travelling together, was particularly impressed by the Emperor's gesture of stepping forward to shake the ex-President's hand. Young wrote that "...such a thing was never before known in the history of Japanese majesty."[3] Alfred, Duke of Edinburgh, who had an audience with the Emperor on his 1869 visit to Japan, and who shook hands with the Emperor a decade earlier, would have been less impressed by the Emperor's gesture to the American. The Duke, however, was of royal blood. Still, the cordiality established by the two leaders was impressive and continued throughout their several meetings during Grant's stay in the Mikado's Empire. The festivities later that day were equally remarkable.

On July 7, the Emperor hosted a military review for the celebrated general, followed by a dinner at Shiba Palace for President and Mrs. Grant. Other guests included Bingham and his wife and British Governor of Hong Kong, John Pope-Hennessy. On July 8, a reception for 1,500 guests was held at the Engineering College, the grandest reception of its kind ever organized for a foreign guest. Financial support for the event was provided in part by donations from leading business leaders *Shibusawa Eiichi* and *Iwasaki Yataro*, scions of Japan's emerging modern capitalist class.[4] Shibusawa founded Japan's first modern bank and established the Tokyo Chamber of Commerce.

Iwasaki founded the Mitsubishi Corporation, created from the remains of business elements of the once powerful *Tosa* domain during Tokugawa rule.

Pope-Hennessy had been the Grant's host in Hong Kong and his presence in Japan on personal travel showed a rift that was developing in British attitudes toward Japan. The split pitted those who favored retention of the unequal treaties, like Parkes, against those who, like Pope-Hennessy, favored revision. His presence also acted as a counterpoint to the decision of the Royal Navy not to join in the naval salute that welcomed Grant's delegation when they entered the port of Yokohama. The division in British policy would become even more apparent in the months and years to come.

In addition to a seemingly endless round of entertainments, the ex-president, escorted by proud Japanese officials, was shown Japan's achievements in areas the Japanese knew Grant cared about deeply: "primary education for both boys and girls; access to economic advancement unrestricted by class, caste, religion, or race; investment in transportation and communications infrastructure, especially railroads; and a willingness to engage in the peaceful settlement of international disputes."[5] And as had been done in Nagasaki, there were tree planting ceremonies. Grant planted a tree near the gate at *Zojoji* in Shiba and both he and Mrs. Grant planted trees in Ueno Park, trees that are all still living.

On July 17, General Grant and his entourage left Tokyo for Nikko, a mountain retreat north of Tokyo, where they spent ten days away from the heat and hubbub of the big city. The interlude was a pleasant one for Grant but not without important business. Home Minister Ito Hirobumi, and Minister of War Saigo Tsugumichi, traveled to Nikko and met with Grant and Bingham. Yoshida also joined the meetings and, as in Grant's meetings with the Emperor, acted as interpreter. Among other issues, the group discussed the status of the Ryukyu Islands and Japan' relations with China.

In China, Grant had met with *Li Hung-chang* (*Li Hongzhang*) China's leading diplomat, to discuss tensions between China and Japan over the Ryukyu Islands. Li was aware of Bingham's influence in Japan as was David McCartee, a former American missionary to China. Attached to the Chinese Legation in Tokyo, McCartee had gone to China as a Presbyterian medical missionary in 1843. He spent 30 years there before relocating to Tokyo where he taught at an institution that later became Tokyo Imperial University. McCartee was known as an excellent linguist and had joined the Chinese legation staff in Japan in 1877.[6] Li also had dealt with Eli Sheppard, Bingham's protégé, during the incident when Japan launched its military expedition to Taiwan early in Bingham's tour. By the time of Grant's visit, Sheppard, at Bingham's recommendation, was also in Tokyo as a key legal advisor to the Japanese government.

Li had suggested the possibility that Grant's good offices could be useful for mitigating, if not resolving, the conflicting claims of Japan and China to the Ryukyu Islands. The Japanese agreed. As a private citizen, Grant was reluctant to take on the task of mediation, but finally assented to serve as an unofficial go-between. The ex-president thought that war between the two Asian powers would only benefit the expansionist designs of western powers, in particular Russia and Great Britain. Grant firmly believed that both China and Japan should be free from foreign domination, a theme he repeatedly emphasized during his cordial visits to both nations. For a time, China and Japan continued to follow up on Grant's discussions. Unfortunately, by the late winter and early spring of 1881, Li Hung-chang and Iwakura

Tomomi had written separately to Grant to tell him that China and
Japan were unable to reconcile their differences. At best, Grant's efforts
may have bought time.[7]

Returning to Tokyo, Grant requested another meeting with the
Emperor and a meeting was arranged for August 10. According to
Donald Keene, who wrote that the Ryukyu issue was mentioned
but not discussed in any detail, Grant used the two-hour occasion
to denounce the attitudes of westerners in Japan in strong terms.[8] In
a letter to his daughter dated the same day, Grant wrote about the
"overbearing and bullying policy of the foreigner and their diplomatic
representatives…" in Japan. He explicitly placed Minister Bingham in
a different category.[9]

Tokyo – The chance concurrence of the cholera scare and the Grant's
visit ironically reinforced the Japanese public feelings toward their new
transpacific diplomatic counterpart. In contrast to other foreign nations,
America's handling of the cholera issue during and after Grant's visit
amplified the already positive atmosphere toward Americans among
Japanese. It also showed a fissure in the foreign community's willingness
to accept Japanese policy. Bingham's Legation, encouraged by the
experience of American missionary doctors, was inclined to trust the
Japanese regulations and the regulators. The Europeans, particularly
the British and Germans, thought the quarantine regulations were
vague. In the summer of 1878, foreign diplomats in Japan had met to
consider a response to Japan's draft quarantine regulations. Sir Harry
Parkes reported to London that all foreign representatives, with the
exception of the American, thought the Japanese regulations were
inadequate. Parkes complained that Bingham "…argued so strongly,
loudly and discourteously in favor of the Revised Regulations…and

in such detail that he must have been privy to the composition."[10] Sir Harry may well have been correct.

Cholera had first come to Japan fifty years earlier and was introduced from the West by way of China. In 1877, there was a particularly virulent epidemic, and, as a result, the Meiji government had stepped up measures to deal with the threat. Dr. D. B. Simmons, who had come to Yokohama as a missionary at the same time as Bingham's interpreter, David Thompson, was at that time advisor to the *Kanagawa* Provincial Government on health matters.[11] The Meiji Government instituted regulations included inspection and quarantine requirements for arriving vessels and were criticized by foreign diplomats. Simmons was well aware of the latest medical knowledge on the spread of cholera and was confident that Japan had been taking sufficient precautions. Other American observers reinforced Bingham's confidence in Japanese quarantine practices. Edward Morse, an American scientist resident in Japan, noted that during the outbreak of cholera in 1877, Japanese containment efforts were significant and highly visible.[12] It was also good politics for the American government to accept the right of the Meiji Government to issue and enforce these regulations. In an argument familiar from earlier squabbles, Sir Harry Parkes held that Japanese regulations did not apply to Her Majesty's subjects. Bingham vigorously disagreed. The disagreement among the western powers in Japan over Japan's cholera regulations had continued while Bingham was on home leave and Durham Stevens, manning the Legation as Charge affaires ad interim, kept the absent minister up to date on developments in Tokyo.[13]

As we have seen, when Grant and his entourage anchored off the coast of Kobe at the end of June, the party respected the quarantine imposed in that region. After Grant had been in Tokyo for two weeks, a German vessel, the *Hesperia* which had not honored the quarantine and had docked at Hyogo (Kobe), arrived off Yokohama. When the Japanese ordered the ship into quarantine, a German doctor came aboard and declared the ship to be free of cholera. The German Minister, Karl von Eisendecher, after consultations with the British and French, told officers of the *Hesperia* to ignore the Japanese government's order and to break the quarantine and unload.[14] Edward House, American editor of the *Tokio Times*, was vociferous in his criticism of the Europeans. Bingham was equally outraged and sent a series of messages to Secretary Evarts blaming the Europeans for the spread of the dread malady to the Yokohama and Tokyo areas.[15] Grant was also upset and made it a point to express his strong condemnation of the German actions. The disagreement within the foreign diplomatic community was clearly on display.

It was convenient and not unreasonable for Americans like House to denounce what they saw as European arrogance. But Europeans were not silent on the issue. Isabella Bird, erstwhile English world traveler and diarist, was a cheerleader for Sir Harry Parkes. Spending several weeks in Hokkaido visiting and living in Ainu communities she wrote in 1878 that the Japanese authorities treated the Ainu "far more favorably than the U.S. Government, for instance, treats the North American Indians."[16] While Bingham may have seen the British as arrogant, many of them saw the Americans as self-righteous.

Disease was unlike some of the other issues that involved Japanese jurisdiction over foreigners. The hunting regulations may have affected a few villagers living around the foreign treaty ports, but for the most part did not concern the broader public. Customs concerns might sometimes have had a general economic impact but did not affect the daily lives of most Japanese. But the Japanese thought of cholera as a

Monument to Grant's visit to Ueno Park. In the background, trees planted by President and Mrs. Grant. Author's photograph.

Grant's Image on Ueno Park monument. Author's photograph.

foreign import and the epidemic had nationwide repercussions. The Japanese language press was also adamant in their condemnation of the *Hesperia*'s violation of the quarantine.[17] As a result, the *Hesperia* incident "fueled the public debate on national sovereignty"[18] in a way that no other issue had before. America's respect for Japan's sovereignty and administrative processes was noticed and appreciated.

As the two-month visit drew near a close on August 25, a public festival was held in Ueno. Attended by the Emperor. the festival celebrated the twelfth anniversary of the move of the capital from Kyoto to Tokyo, but also served as a convenient occasion to honor the American visitor.[19] Following just three years after Japan's successful participation in the Philadelphia Centennial Exposition, heavy coverage of Grant's visit in the American press further cemented Japan's positive image in the minds of the American public. The months of July and August in 1879 were undoubtedly one of the high points of good feeling in the bilateral relationship

Grant's discussions with the Emperor and other high-level Japanese officials reinforced the policies Bingham had been advocating since he first arrived. Grant expressed "warmest wishes for the independence of Japan," and added "We have great interests in the Pacific, but we have none that are inconsistent with the independence of these nations."[20] Among the many issues he addressed he spoke about America's policy regarding the unequal treaties and insisted that Japan not rely on external debt in its search for resources to fund national development. Bingham was particularly pleased that Grant had raised with the Emperor the possibility of creation of a national legislative assembly. The multiple opportunities to participate in social events and policy meetings at the most senior level raised Bingham's and the Legation's profile within the diplomatic community and among Japanese officials

And Grant and his party took back to the States an appreciation for what Bingham had accomplished in building the Legation into an effective institution.

Chapter Fourteen
New Arrivals, New Perspectives

Tokyo - Grant's visit had provided an opportunity to advance America's policy interests and an occasion to examine the ever-evolving relationship between the Japanese and American people. Bingham's hard work to maximize the positive impact of former President Grant's visit was largely successful. Japan's enthusiastic reception of Grant and his wife, Julia, resonated with the largely positive coverage of the Japan sojourn in the American press. Grant was not a head of state but had been. And there was serious talk that he might run again for a third term.

As the Meiji Restoration continued transforming Japan, the attitudes of foreigners and the policies of foreign governments were also changing. When Count Iwakura met with President Grant at the White House in 1872, his mission had been to push for revision of the unequal treaties. When he greeted Grant at the dock in Yokohama, just seven years later, he still retained that hope as Japan had made remarkable advancements in the intervening years. Bingham had been on hand to observe these developments and to guide America's policy during this dynamic period. He realized that Japanese were becoming more nuanced in their understanding of America's politics and culture and that the American resident community in Japan was diversifying. He watched and helped to influence a change in European attitudes on issues he had championed and which was beginning to see results. But he worried about anti-Asian racial sentiment back home. It was a prejudice he had fought against since Oregon's admission to the Union twenty years earlier. The ugliness now threatened to poison American diplomacy within East Asia.

Tokyo – Despite shifts in the make-up of the foreign community in Japan, Bingham was able to maintain a good working relationship with the more prominent members of American expatriate society. The social environment that had greeted Bingham's arrival in 1873 was quite different by 1879. Now familiarity with America among the Japanese was growing. An increasing number of Japanese had traveled overseas. Students in Tokyo, Yokohama and even provincial cities were learning western languages. The number of Japanese studying abroad was impressive. From the mid-1860s to 1880 approximately 40 Japanese students studied at Rutgers University in New Jersey alone. Multiplied by dozens of other institutions of higher learning, and added to the Japanese studying in Europe or at western style schools in Japan, the number of western-trained Japanese was considerable. At the same time, the Meiji government's use of *oyatoi gaikokujin* or foreign experts, continued to be a factor in promoting interaction among Japanese and Americans. By the 1880s the portion of such experts hired by the Japanese government was decreasing but was compensated by increased hiring of foreigners by newly emerging private sector commercial and industrial organizations. This meant an expanded environment for social mixing.

During Bingham's first months in Tokyo, his primary American contacts had been with a small group of Protestant missionaries and a handful of businessmen and American officials hired by the Meiji government. By the time of the Grant visit, there was a growing presence of new Americans. Among these were scholars and young and adventuresome Americans who were eager to immerse themselves in Japanese culture and were keen to share their infatuation with Japan with cities back home, like Boston and New York. Missionaries from denominations other than the Presbyterians and Reformed groups had become active. This diversification, while not wholly unwelcome, did make the American community Bingham represented more like America as a whole and less like his comfortable hometown of Cadiz.

Notable among the early arrivals of secular intellectuals was a young scientist from New England, Edward Sylvester Morse. As a young scholar, Morse was invited to work with noted Harvard University zoologist, Louis Agassiz, who at the time was "carrying on his doomed intellectual battle with Charles Darwin..."[1] When Dr. David Murray met Morse at the Philadelphia Exhibition in 1876, he had been impressed by the young scientist and had invited Morse to come to Japan to lecture on Darwinism. Morse noticed an unusual shell deposit at a site along the railroad between Yokohama and Tokyo. This discovery led him to begin the first archeological excavation in Japan and to open up a new chapter in the study of Japan's national origins. While in Japan, Morse became friends with journalist Edward House[2] and Charles LeGendre. The latter had an intense interest in the origins of the Japanese people and from time to time joined Morse at the archeological dig.[3]

At the advice of his physician, Morse began taking long walks through the streets of Tokyo. With an artist's eye, and a collector's passion, he became entranced by the details of Japanese life. Keeping an illustrated diary, Morse compiled a sympathetic treatment of the intricacies of Japanese daily life and craftsmanship. As members of the American community, Morse and his family participated actively in Japanese life. Morse mentioned General Grant speaking with his young daughter at a dinner and reception for the visiting ex-president at Ueno Park. The episode, he wrote, altered his negative opinion of the general which he had formed by reading "the infernal slanders of our newspapers."[4] Morse had been instrumental in bringing another American intellectual, Ernest Fenollosa to Japan. The recent Harvard graduate and fledgling art historian began lecturing at the University of Tokyo in 1878 on "the history of philosophy from Descartes to Hegel."[5] When Morse returned to New England in 1880, he became an enthusiastic messenger for the wonders of Japan.[6] Both at home and in Japan, the Reverend John Walker's approach to the sweep of history, so influential in Bingham's early education, was being challenged by a seductive secular interpretation.

Morse's lectures on Darwin and Fenollosa's lectures on Spencer were an important factor in promoting a growing recognition in Japan that not all westerners believed Christianity was a necessary prerequisite for Japan's economic and social advancement. Darwin's *On the Origin of Species* was available in English in Japanese bookstores as early as 1876. In 1881, the same year that the Japanese translation of *The New Testament* was published, a Japanese translation of *The Descent of Man*, was available.[7] The latter was translated by *Kozu Senzaburo* who had gone to study in America on the recommendation of David Murray. Herbert Spencer's influential *Social Statics*, first published in 1851, was available in translation by 1882. While the missionaries were still managing to feed Japan's appetite for Christian texts; the Japanese themselves were nourishing Japanese thinkers with new

145

imported ideas to feed a ravenous intellectual hunger.

As he had with Morse, Bingham maintained a cordial relationship with Fenollosa, but he did feel it was useful to put down a modest marker that acceptance of science need not mean a rejection of the Christian faith. Fenollosa and other intellectuals were active in the Asiatic Society, along with Dr. James Hepburn and Dr. David Murray. Bingham had become a member of the Society shortly after his arrival in Japan but there is little evidence of his active participation in this scholarly group. He did, however, along with Sir Harry Parkes and Dr. David Murray, become a founding member of the Tokio Christian Association, formed in the late 1870s. The group's charter was to pursue intellectual interests in an open atmosphere but still within a Christian context. To do that, the association established a reading room and lecture program. Sir Harry Parkes was the association's largest donor. Bingham and David Murray were the next most charitable benefactors.[8]

Despite his close working relationship with many of the Protestant missionaries, congeniality did not guarantee agreement on intellectual and political matters. In general, Bingham's stance on many policy issues fit better with Secretary of State Evarts' political world than his nephew's religious one. Daniel Crosby Green, was a quiet, studious type. Green had been in Japan as a missionary since 1869 and had worked in Kobe until 1874 before moving to Yokohama in 1880 to work on the translation of *The New Testament* into Japanese. Green, like his uncle, came from the elite sector of eastern society that had proven an important source of political collaborators throughout Bingham's congressional career.[9] The Evarts family had been involved in the American Board of Commissioners of Foreign Missionaries since the early nineteenth century and Green was the first missionary assigned overseas after the Board's reorganization. Critical of Bingham's style generally, Green wrote to a friend in praise of the Minister's strong stance in supporting the Japanese on the cholera issue. "I can almost forget his crude notions of political economy in view of his maintaining so vigorous a stand for the rights of the Japanese government".[10]

Green's comments on Bingham's "crude notions" like Dr. Murray's wife's description of the Binghams as very "Ohio" showed that eastern social snobbery crossed the Pacific with Americans. In 1879 Bingham hosted a departure dinner for Dr. David Murray. Murray's influence as educational advisor to the Japanese government had been immense. And although his wife may have looked down her nose a bit at the Ohio Binghams, the professional relationship of the educator and the diplomat was productive. In speaking at a dinner honoring the New Jersey educator, Bingham used Murray's example to extoll personal and institutional cooperation between Japan and the United States.[11] It was also an example of Bingham's ability to bridge the gap between Franklin College in New Athens, Ohio, and Rutgers, Yale, and Harvard in the East.

Bingham was fully aware of new currents that were watering intellectual life in Japan, but he retained his firm belief, whatever science might teach, that America's constitutional government of the people was the culmination of a divine purpose. He did not worry about whether this divine purpose might be facilitated by the struggle of the fittest to survive or the expression of a sociological dialectic. Interestingly, David Thompson kept a personal notebook which showed an open-minded interest in the newest scientific and theological developments.[12] A warm letter from close friend Lewis Lawton in Cadiz described how he saw Bingham's service in Japan. "I have never looked upon on you as merely the political agent and representative of our Government to the government of Japan, but regard you and your family as a sort of missionaries also to their people, of all that is good in the civilization of our free country."[13] Undoubtedly, Bingham appreciated these words.

The Grant visit also brought American and European policy differences into relief. By taking a firm stand on affirming Japan's handling of the cholera outbreak, America showed principled sympathy for Japanese autonomy on a vital and visible issue. Coupled with the 1877 Convention agreement, the Meiji government could hope that the Europeans would see the value of following the American example. During and after Grant's stay in Japan, Bingham moved to reinforce this potential policy shift.

From mid-August to early November, 1879, the *Japan Weekly Mail* ran a series of articles which provided exhaustive historical detail of the development of the concept of extraterritoriality in western history. The series began with discussion of the immunity of Roman citizens to local laws in that ancient civilization. In June of that year, the *Mail* had run an editorial saying the paper had no objection to the fact that talks about revising the unequal treaties were underway. The author of the series "Extraterritoriality in Japan" was Eli T. Sheppard, John Bingham's one-time ear on the State Department and now an important eye on the Ministry of Foreign Affairs. Now, Bingham's former Ohio colleague became a supportive voice in the local press. Dr. John Walker of Franklin College would have recognized and applauded the analysis. And the contemporary reader would have known that Sheppard had coordinated closely with his minister in preparing the series.

Significantly, with the Hong Kong governor visiting Japan at the time of Grant's Japan visit, the *Hesperia* incident had exposed a rift in

British opinion. The issue of the applicability of Japanese regulations to British subjects was already under discussion within the British government. Hong Kong Governor Pope-Hennessy, who had come to Japan during the former president's visit, criticized Parkes' stance on the issue, an opinion that was echoed by many in the foreign community in Japan. That the *Japan Weekly Mail*, which was pro-British on many issues, joined the criticism against the European flaunting of Japanese quarantine rules, showed the major shift in European attitudes and

Monument at site of Omori Shell Mound in Shinagawa-ku, Tokyo, where Dr. Edward Morse discovered prehistoric shell middens. Author's photograph.

a convergence with the American approach. Throughout his career, Pope-Hennessy was criticized by many British for being too pro-native. But now, Parkes' heyday as the leading advocate of the western powers' privileged status in Japan was drawing to a close.

San Francisco - Returning from his worldwide tour, Grant was dismayed by the contrast with the Asia he had visited and the ignorance and racism toward Asia among Americans. In 1871 Bingham had seen this racism when he traveled to California and Oregon to campaign in support of Republican candidates and civil rights enforcement legislation. Eight years later, writing from San Francisco to thank Bingham for his work in Japan, Grant decried the lack of interest among Americans about Japan, "The fact is the people here are so absorbed with their Anti-Chinese discussions that they hardly know there is such a country that one has to pass to reach the territory of their aversion."[14] Although later in the same letter, Grant did say that he anticipated Americans' interest in Japan would increase; it is clear that the health of America's bilateral ties with Japan was not immune to racism. In 1878, President Hayes had vetoed legislation that would have prohibited Chinese immigration, but in 1882, President Arthur signed the Chinese Exclusion Act. The Act did not specifically target Japanese. For that, there would be future American government actions.

Bingham clearly recognized that the Chinese Exclusion Act made progress in the relationship with Japan more difficult. The Electoral College Compromise of 1877 and Supreme Court decisions had earlier gutted Bingham's intended impact of the 14th amendment. Now anti-Asian racism jeopardized his efforts to build America's stature as a reliable partner to Japan. In Bingham's view such negative developments were set-backs, not defeat. There was work to be done and his commitment to constitutional law and to God's eventual justice remained firm. Bingham was anxious to take advantage of the afterglow of Grant's visit. But passage of the Act reminded Japanese officials that even if America was not aiming at them directly, some American politicians would not hesitate to shoot in their direction.

Chapter Fifteen

Presidential Transition and Tragedy

Tokyo - As he approached his sixty-fifth birthday on January 21, 1880, Bingham looked toward to the fall election and wanted to continue to serve. He was healthy and believed there was still important work he could do. But it was an election year, and his future depended first on the outcome of the Republican party convention and then of the fall election. If 1876 was any guide, neither would be easy.

Bingham was aware that there would be competition to replace him as minister to Japan, even if a sympathetic Republican were elected. Even before Bingham took home leave, Eli Sheppard had brought gossip from Washington that confirmed the minister's fears that Van Buren was trying to undermine Bingham's work in Japan and was angling to take his position.[1] Naval Officer J. Barton, whom Bingham had recommended for his Washington assignment and who had provided information to Bingham about prospects in the Hayes administration, continued to serve Bingham as a reliable mole in the corridors of the capital. Barton informed Bingham that key players in Washington shared an annoyance with Van Buren.[2] Still, Bingham had no doubts that Van Buren was not the only aspirant.

As the Republican convention got underway in June, there were three strong candidates, former Present Grant, seeking an unprecedented third term, John Sherman of Ohio and James Blaine of Maine. Bingham was confident Grant would offer him an appointment, but he was not certain it would be in Japan. Sherman would be lukewarm to Bingham. As fellow Ohioans, the two men knew each other well but were not close. A Blaine presidency was unpredictable. Blaine had been speaker of the house in Bingham's later years in Congress, and they shared a general political outlook. But Blaine had no obligations to his old fellow House member. When the convention dead-locked and turned to Ohio Representative James Garfield on the thirty-sixth ballot, Bingham was suddenly optimistic.

With Garfield's win in the general election, the competition to fill the Japan minister slot began. In the month before his inauguration, Garfield had received a letter from Grant, recommending that Bingham be promoted to the American mission to Austria. Grant suggested that John Russell Young, traveling companion on his world tour, be assigned to Tokyo. Grant's justification for the change was that while Bingham was an admirable representative, Young would prove more energetic.[3] Young had lobbied Grant for the Tokyo job, and both he and journalist Edward House shared the opinion that Bingham was too low energy. Young had arranged for House to meet with Grant during the ex-president's stay in Tokyo. It was an opportunity for House to get to know Grant and to pass along Young's interest in the Tokyo position.[4] House also stayed at the Grant's residence in Galena, Illinois, for three days when he returned to the States in 1880.[5] In the same letter to Garfield in which he recommended Young, Grant wrote that with regard to the Yokohama Consulate General, Van Buren "… should not be allowed to remain there a moment longer than can be helped."[6] Grant recognized that Van Buren's powerful supporters could make removal controversial but felt House would be an excellent choice for the Yokohama position. Despite this maneuvering, both Bingham and Van Buren retained their posts.

Garfield recognized in Bingham a kindred spirit on returning the Shimonoseki Indemnity, and, as an Ohio politician realized the growing importance of the kerosene trade that had become America's main export to Japan. The Rockefeller refinery was in Cleveland, and the oil was in the ground in eastern Ohio and western Pennsylvania. Garfield had little incentive to move Bingham, and there was an opening in Beijing that Young could fill. Van Buren was not welcome anywhere else, but it was useful to keep his New Jersey supporters quiet and his own meddlesome voice far away in Yokohama. When Garfield asked Blaine to serve as secretary of state, Bingham was confident of a receptive and sympathetic ear in Washington, one that should facilitate his push on the indemnity and treaty issues. Blaine could also lend backup to Bingham's effort to take advantage of new commercial opportunities.

Washington, Tokyo, Seoul (*Hanyang*) - Before turning to address the indemnity and treaty issues once again, Bingham had to deal with an international crisis involving Japan's relationship to its Asian neighbors. In East Asia, the political distinctions had become even more stark, and traditional cultural differences now took on modern nationalist trappings. Koreans often describe their peninsula as a shrimp between two whales. The whales are the often-competing interests of Japan and China. As the nineteenth century entered its final decades, Russian, British, and American whales also churned the surrounding waters. In Tokyo, the diplomatic community that welcomed the new decade in Japan was no longer solely Western. Both the Chinese and Korean delegations were well established and presented new challenges. For Bingham, continued peace in the region remained his hope. For some in Washington, there were other ambitions.

In April of 1880, Commodore Robert Shufeldt, commander of the *USS Ticonderoga* arrived in Nagasaki. The United States Navy and the Department of State had agreed to send Shufeldt on a diplomatic mission to East Asia. The mission was to include a stop in Korea. Japan had signed a treaty with Korea in 1876 and was the only nation to recognize Korea as an independent nation, not a dependency of China. This had put Japan in an advantageous but awkward position with the other powers in the region. Mindful of Japanese sensitivities, Hayes' Secretary of State Evarts had instructed the Navy Department to request that Bingham first approach the Japanese Ministry of Foreign Affairs to provide official letters of introduction to Korean authorities. At the Foreign Ministry, *Inoyue Kaoru*[7] was unwilling to provide such letters but did agree to introduce Shufeldt to the Japanese consul in Pusan who would act as an intermediary. When the Koreans would not agree to forward Shufeldt's message to Seoul, he became suspicious. The Japanese, Shufeldt thought, were not helping arrange a channel to communicate with Seoul in order to maintain their position of privilege in Korea. Instead of assisting they were actively blocking the American overture to the Korean court.[8]

While in Nagasaki awaiting developments, Shufeldt had gotten to know the Chinese consul and arranged to contact the *Tsungli Yamen*, the organ of the Ching (Qing) government that handled foreign affairs. Shufeldt then returned to the United States, where back in Washington he was able to renew his campaign to contact Korea. And this time, with the Garfield Administration now in power, he was working with a new cabinet. He still had the same minister in Tokyo, though, and Bingham's counsel was to approach Korea through Japan. Shufeldt preferred the Chinese channel. It was not the last time that the diplomatic mission in Japan would take a different approach than that of the American military.

Bingham was hopeful that Japan could play a positive role in bringing Korea into the international family of nations. When Garfield's Secretary of State James Blaine accepted Shufeldt's plan to operate out of China as he approached Korea, Bingham felt it was important to keep Japan involved. He suggested that Korea send a representative to Tokyo and that this representative be authorized to negotiate a treaty. This idea "annoyed" China's Li Hung-chang.[9] When Shufeldt arrived at Inchon to meet with the Koreans, he was greeted by a Japanese gunboat, *Banjo*, which delivered a letter to Shufeldt from Bingham introducing him to Hanabusa Yoshitada, Japan's senior official in Korea. But Japan's willingness to assist the United States in its approach to Korea had come too late.[10] Bingham's initiative was a dead letter. Shufeldt was already negotiating with Korea through Chinese channels.

Shufeldt waited patiently in Tientsin (Tianjin) until the end of 1881, when the Koreans finally indicated a willingness to talk, and by May of 1882 the United States and Korea entered into the Treaty of Amity, Commerce and Navigation, the first western nation to do so. Other treaties with foreign powers followed: the British and Germans in 1883, Russia in 1884 and France in 1886. For the Chinese, the policy of diluting Japanese influence in Korea by involving the other foreign powers had worked. For America, the policy of support for independent nations open to foreign commerce had been extended to a small but geographically important market. In a letter to former President Grant just after his arrival in China as minister, John Russell

Young wrote critically about the treaty. "Our treaty," Young told Grant, "however, was a Chinese measure. Li planned it, practically wrote it, and ordered the Coreans to sign it."[11] Young was concerned that China, humiliated by Japan by the earlier incursion into Taiwan, by Japan's successfully claiming the Ryukyu Islands, and now, meddling in Korea, would provoke a war. Young echoed Grant and other Americans in believing that a war would weaken both China and Japan leaving northeast Asia at the mercy of Great Britain and Russia.

For Bingham, who held a positive view of the modernizing role Japan might play in the region, events in Korea immediately following the signing of the Korean-American treaty gave room for optimism. But the situation was still volatile. In the summer of 1882, Korean troops rioted in Seoul. In the ensuing melee, the Japanese Legation was destroyed, and Japanese diplomats were forced to flee. Bingham was impressed by Japan's restrained handling of the sensitive incident which mixed Korean domestic factional politics with international intrigue. Additionally, the American minister was satisfied with the terms of the Japan-Korea Treaty of 1882, although he had been outmaneuvered by Shufeldt and the Chinese in the negotiating process.

In 1883, Bingham held several meetings with Korean progressive *Kim Ok-kyun*. Kim had studied at *Fukuzawa Yukichi's* Keio University and was among a group of Korean nationalists pushing for modernization on the Meiji model. Kim's original purpose was to secure a loan with the aid of Yokohama businessman James R. Morse. Morse traveled to New York to secure the loan, but, after failing, decided to use this new channel to sell goods to Korea. His primary business was watches and clocks, but by the next year, Korea had bought 4,000 rifles and a number of Gatlin guns through Morse. The American government role in the arms sale was likely tangential.

But it does illustrate that Bingham's Legation saw the Meiji model as beneficial for Korea and was comfortable dealing with pro-Japanese Koreans. Bingham was further pleased in 1884 when Japan forgave the indemnity the initial bilateral treaty had imposed on Korea.[12]

Then, just months before leaving his post in Tokyo, John Bingham met with Ito Hirobumi to discuss Korea. Ito was preparing to travel to China to meet with Li Hung-chang for talks about Korea, and sought Bingham's advice. Bingham told Ito that China and Japan should agree to withdraw their troops from Korea and that any war between the two Asian nations would be disastrous for both. Whether convinced by Bingham's suggestion or concerned that the recent resolution of China's conflict with France in Indochina made China a more formidable adversary, Japan agreed in the Li-Ito agreement to resolve affairs peacefully, at least for the moment.[13] Consequently, by the time he left Japan in 1885, Bingham felt positive about the direction of Japan's relationship with China. Subsequent events would make Bingham's attitude appear naïve. But Hilary Conroy's classic, *The Japanese Seizure of Korea*, would help provide a corrective. In a statement that might excuse, if not defend, Bingham's point of view, Conroy wrote that Japan's policy at the time was "...too inconsistent, and yes blundering...to be characterized as an organized scheme to take over Korea."[14] During his final years in Tokyo, Japan and the United States had both increased their influence in the region. But influence did not mean control. In 1885, as Bingham was leaving Japan, Japanese policy toward Korea was in flux. It still is.

CHAPTER SIXTEEN

Policy Progress Amid Racial Tension

Washington, D.C. - Tragically, Garfield and Blaine's tenure was brief, and its impact on America's Japan policy, minimal. Four months after Garfield's inauguration, on July 2, 1881, Blaine's State Department carriage stopped by the White House. Blaine was escorting the president on the short ride to Potomac Station. At the station, Garfield was to board a train for New England to attend his 25th class reunion at Williams College in Massachusetts.[1] At the station, Garfield was shot and severely wounded by Charles Guiteau, a mentally unstable and frustrated office seeker. Garfield did not die until September 19.

In December, Grant weighed in again with Garfield's replacement, Chester Arthur of New York, suggesting Young for the Tokyo post and once again urging removal of Van Buren, whom Arthur retained in Yokohama. Grant spoke highly of Bingham but understood at the time that Bingham was to be appointed as one of two foreigners on a five-judge Japanese superior court that was being formed.[2] Arthur decided to keep Bingham in Japan and appointed Young to Beijing. Unsurprisingly, the idea for a Superior Court with both Japanese and foreign judges never materialized. Frederick Frelinghuysen of New Jersey took Blaine's spot as secretary of state. Frelinghuysen, as a senator from New Jersey, had voted guilty in the Andrew Johnson impeachment and later served as Chairman of the Senate Foreign Relations Committee.

Tokyo - Secure in his position in Tokyo, Bingham continued to push his cherished policy initiatives and made considerable progress in advocating for American business and in upgrading the Legation. Under the Arthur administration there was no major change in Washington policy towards Japan but the mood of American involvement in East Asia continued to evolve. Bingham had enjoyed a close personal tie to Garfield and the recently assassinated leader had been an important champion of the Shimonoseki Indemnity issue in the House. Arthur, however, was quite a different person. In 1882 Arthur signed the Chinese Exclusion Act. Although it did not specifically target Japanese immigration, Japanese officials knew that the mood in America was ominous.

Bingham's retention promised continuity in important policy initiatives he had spearheaded, including on the unequal treaties and return of the Shimonoseki Indemnity. It also meant Washington could remain confident of the effectiveness of Legation management and reassured that in a region growing ever more contentious America had a seasoned, steady leader in place in Tokyo. At the Japanese Foreign Ministry, Inoyue Kaoru had succeeded Terashima Munenori, whose position had been shaky in the wake of his handling of the cholera issue. In January of 1880 Henry Denison succeeded Eli Sheppard as legal advisor to the Ministry of Foreign Affairs. These developments further cemented the American Legation's personal connections with the Ministry. The *Tokio Times* noted on May 8, 1880, that Sheppard had paid a courtesy departure call on the Emperor, evidence of the esteem in which this advisory position was held.[3]

California, Washington - Bingham's push on the treaty revision and Shimonoseki Indemnity issues continued to lumber along. The policy direction was clear, but the lack of speed was frustrating. Now more than ever, though, he had an ally in Edward House of the *Tokio Times*. In August, 1880, House had returned to America from Japan after closing down the *Tokio Times*. In its final months of publication, the English-language, pro-American *Times* had sponsored an essay contest open to its subscribers. Prizes were offered to writers who contributed articles on revising of the unequal treaties.[4]

From the time he reached California on August 19, House was "imbued with a mission." A friend of Grant's and Mark Twain, his mission had four goals: "broader American sympathies for Japan, the return of the United States' portion of the Shimonoseki Indemnity, revision of the treaties and the recall of British Minister Harry Parkes."[5] House's campaign to return the Shimonoseki Indemnity and Grant's support for such a move reflected a strong current in American political attitudes toward Japan; the consensus had come around to the position Bingham had been advocating for a decade.

Few diplomats in the field at the time understood as well as Bingham why it took Congress so long to resolve these issues. In his December 1879 address, President Hayes had recommended return of the indemnity payments and both the House and the Senate favored return of funds to the Japanese. Naturally, there were discussions and disagreements over details but there was general agreement that returning at least a major portion of the money paid by the Japanese was the right thing to do.

Washington, Poughkeepsie, New York - During Arthur's presidency, momentum accelerated on the two overarching policy issues that had long dominated America's relationship with Japan. Resolution of the Shimonoseki Indemnity occurred first and took place while Bingham was still serving in Japan. During Bingham's final months in Congress, in the lame duck session of 1873, a petition from American religious and academic leaders had called on Congress to return the indemnity to Japan. In 1883, a similar effort added a theatrical touch. Birdsey Northrup, a prominent educator who had met with Mori Arinori when the Iwakura Mission was in the States, had been a tireless supporter of indemnity return. Northrup was present to hand over to Congress "a 40-foot long petition signed by virtually every influential figure in academia and the clergy in the U.S."[6]

It had been a full decade since Bingham's initial skirmish with British Minister Parkes over acceptance of Shimonoseki Indemnity payments. By the Spring of 1883, even the *Japan Mail* had admitted that the encounter in the Shimonoseki Straits and the resultant indemnity demands had not been justified. Then in a message dated March 21, Bingham was informed by Secretary of State Frelinghuysen that the Congress had voted to return the indemnity. For Bingham, who believed that American diplomatic policy would prove practical if founded on moral principles, this resolution was providential. America had done the right thing and at the same time had gained favor and appreciation from the Japanese government. As a concrete expression of that appreciation, Japan agreed to provide favorable terms for American occupation of the parcel of land in Tokyo where the Embassy and the Ambassador's residence is now located.[7]

Treaty revision proved more cumbersome; the blockage was in Washington, not Tokyo. When Britain proposed a joint conference on treaty revision to be held in Tokyo in 1879, Bingham initially had indicated he would not attend. Evarts had held that the 1878 Evarts-Yoshida Convention was sufficient and instructed Bingham not to participate. The issue remained stagnant until another call to convene a conference in Tokyo was brought forward by the Japanese government. The conference was scheduled to take place in 1882. As Evarts had done before, President Garfield's Secretary of State James Blaine instructed Bingham not to attend a conference on the issue. However, when Blaine resigned after Garfield's assassination, Bingham renewed his request to new Secretary of State Frederick Frelinghuysen that he be allowed to attend the 1882 conference as an observer. The secretary granted Bingham's request.[8]

Bingham protégé Henry Denison, now an advisor to the Ministry of Foreign Affairs and successor to Eli Sheppard in that role, played an important part in drafting the proposed revisions.[9] But when the draft was brought forward by Foreign Minister Inyoue, Bingham took exception to some proposed import tariff changes which he felt penalized the United States and favored the British. Consequently, Bingham boycotted some of the conference sessions.[10] When Sir Harry Parkes returned to Tokyo at the beginning of the year, after an extended stay in London, Bingham's initiatives once again faced a more formidable opponent. By early summer the talks which had begun at the first of the year had deadlocked.

While in Tokyo, Bingham sought to attract European support for treaty revision by using an information campaign in the local press, the Japanese Legation in Washington was employing a similar strategy to appeal to the American public. Representative of Japan's multi-dimensional approach was the successful media coverage of a young Japanese woman's graduation from Vassar College. *Yamakawa*

Sutematsu was one of five young Japanese women who had accompanied the Iwakura Mission and had stayed in America to study. Birdsey Northrup, the Connecticut educator and leader on the Shimonoseki Indemnity issue, had taken several of these young women under his care. The youngest, six-year-old *Tsuda Ume*[11], was placed with a family in Georgetown.

For a decade, Yamakawa had been folded into the embrace of the missionary/educational environment in the United States that was so influential to the bilateral relationship in the 1870s.[12] Speaking at her college graduation ceremony, her address was entitled, "British Policy

Yamakawa Sutematsu. Photo courtesy Vassar College archives.

Toward Japan." Reports of the speech were picked up by newspapers around the country. The *New York Times* in its June 14, 1882, edition wrote that "She thoroughly understood England's conservatism, and paid tribute to America's liberality and friendship."[13] Japanese Consul in New York, *Takaki Saburo* had attended the graduation ceremony. The graduation was more than a personal celebration for the young graduate; the speech was a diplomatic triumph.

In addition to the sustained media campaign in both capitals, Bingham continued placing key mentors in influential positions In 1883, Durham W. Stevens left his post as deputy at the Legation in Tokyo to take a position with the Japanese Legation in Washington. Stevens' contributions to these efforts were no doubt significant. In June of 1883, Parkes left Japan permanently to take an assignment as Her Majesty's Minister to China. And at the end of 1883 in his annual report to the Congress, President Arthur said it was time to revise the treaty with Japan. Bingham's long cherished goal of revision of the unequal treaties appeared to be within reach. Unfortunately, any resolution languished in Congress until the Senate took action in 1899, well beyond Bingham's departure from Japan.[14] Still, he remained confident that in time, Japan would achieve the equality among nations that he had cultivated so long and so assiduously.

CHAPTER SEVENTEEN

Promoting American Business

Tokyo - Since arriving in Japan, Bingham had been eager to promote American commercial interests, and during the second part of his service his efforts had begun to show results. Still, despite the warm feelings on both sides generated by President Grant's visit, American business interest in Japan remained modest. Trade with Japan was scarcely two percent of America's total world trade. Annual two-way trade in the years between Bingham's arrival in 1873 and his return from home leave in 1879 hovered around $10 million, and trade volume did not increase appreciably in the early 1880s. Moreover, the imbalance continued to favor Japan.[1] Between 1875 and 1880, there was a modest growth in the number of Americans resident in the treaty ports, from 353 to 407. Overall western population in foreign residential areas shrunk from 3,583 to 2,359, perhaps because more foreigners were living outside the treaty port limits, in Tokyo, in particular.[2] When figures became available for Chinese residents in 1880, these showed the total to be one-third more than the total of all western residents of any nationality.

American merchants were often dependent on Chinese middlemen and had begun to face increased competition from a burgeoning cadre of Japanese entrepreneurs. Shipping records show large numbers of Chinese passengers crossing the Pacific in steerage. But there were also Chinese merchants in first class. In the words of historian Kevin Murphy, "American merchants were reduced to little more than always irritable, if sometimes well-paid, spectators…as their Asian 'servants' controlled the essential aspects of their trade, paying themselves largely as they saw fit and as the market allowed."[3] While looking at the more recent impact of western culture on Japan, it is important to recognize that China's relationship with Japan was as vital in Bingham's time as it was in the previous centuries and as it is now.

New Japanese enterprises were often supported by the Meiji government and aimed to become direct competitors with foreign firms. By 1880 such groups as Yasuda Mutual Life Company and

Photograph shows Chinese in Yokohama in Bingham's time.
Photo Courtesy of the Yokohama Archives of History.

Mitsui Bank were well established. The Mitsubishi group, for example, was active in shipping and ship repair. Young entrepreneur Shibusawa Eiichi, who went on to help found hundreds of companies as well as the Tokyo Chamber of Commerce, and others like him, had become important actors in the Meiji commercial world.

Commercial diplomacy was not only the promotion of national products, it also entailed policy work to ensure equitable market access. In 1881, John Bingham played an important role in mediating a dispute between foreign merchants in the silk trade and their increasingly assertive Japanese suppliers. In September, a group of seventy foreign silk merchants met at the German Club in Yokohama to draft a resolution expressing their "disappointment and astonishment" at the formation of the Japanese Silk Guild.[4] According to its bylaws, the silk business in Japan was to be divided into three elements. The first were sorting companies, suppliers located in the provinces who collected material from local producers. The suppliers then provided product to a storage company in the port. The final element was commission merchants, the group who had been the primary organizers of the guild. In Japan, the Silk Guild argued, in contrast to practice in other markets, foreign entities controlled the intermediate stage of the supply chain, the premises where the silk was stored, inspected and payment arranged. The Guild held that this practice disadvantaged Japanese sellers and that there should be a public auction facility to ensure fairness between buyer and seller.[5] The dispute halted and threatened longer term disruption of the silk trade, the most important commodity in Japan's external trade.

Bingham's role as mediator of this dispute marked an important milestone in Japanese commercial institutional development. As dean of the diplomatic corps in Sir Harry Parkes' absence, and because he was respected by both Japanese and foreign disputants, Bingham arranged to have both sides meet at the American Legation. Shibusawa Eiichi, whom Bingham knew well, was an important leader on the Japanese side. Shibusawa had played a key role in organizing many of the events during Grant's visit so had been in regular contact with the American Legation in planning details of the visit. Shibusawa was joined at the talks by Mitsui Bussan's *Masuda Takashi*.[6] The most prominent foreign merchant participants were American businessman Thomas Walsh, and A.J. Wilkin, an Australian. Bingham had known Walsh since his initial crossing from San Francisco to Yokohama in 1873. Wilkin was a prominent lay member of Yokohama Union Church.[7] The foreign side insisted that the inspection system at the foreign companies' facilities had been necessary because of Japanese fraud. Further, the Japanese attempt to change the system without prior consultation was unacceptable. The argument was bitter and the press coverage characteristically histrionic. But with Bingham as mediator both sides were able to settle and publish an agreement in mid-November which acknowledged the role of both parties in creation and operation of a neutral facility at the intermediate stage of the supply chain.[8] Once again, Bingham had found a middle way.

On another trade issue Bingham was not interested in satisfying all sides; he wanted to protect American interests. The issue was America's sales of kerosene in the Japanese market. By the last quarter of the 19th century, kerosene had almost entirely displaced whale oil as a source for illumination. In Japan, by value, kerosene made up half of all American imports. And Legation efforts to maintain favorable tariffs on kerosene and block regulations on storage that would disadvantage American suppliers, preoccupied Bingham and his staff.

Bingham knew the industry well. In Ohio, commercial interest in kerosene export was a political force. Bingham's old House district in eastern Ohio and his childhood home of Mercer, Pennsylvania, were close to oil-rich areas. In the 1870s, John D. Rockefeller had been buying up wells in western Pennsylvania and had built a refinery at Cleveland. Rockefeller's burgeoning business pushed to influence American policy. Both Hayes and Garfield, as Ohio politicians, wanted a thriving kerosene industry which meant fair treatment in the Japanese market. While it is not certain just what financial support these two presidents might have had from "Big Kerosene", such backing was a subject of political discussion. Historian Ron Chernow wrote, "Garfield was the first of many presidential contenders who grappled with the quandary of whether it made better sense to court Rockefeller's money or capitalize on public animosity against him."[9] Bingham had no hesitation; he unequivocally supported the interests of American kerosene imports into Japan.

Hokkaido, Pittsburgh – Another area on which Bingham concentrated was railroads. Tariffs were and still are not the only factor that can impede or distort trade. Standards are also equally, if not even more, crucial. Beginning with the opening of the Yokohama to Tokyo line in 1877, the British had dominated the railroad business in Japan. This meant rail construction and equipment was to British standards. Prior to Bingham's term in Japan, his predecessor Charles DeLong had tried to sell American railroad knowhow to Japan. His efforts had been unsuccessful.[10]

In Philadelphia at the Centennial Exhibition, American railroad prowess had been on display. Baldwin Locomotive Works, based in Philadelphia, had had an impressive presence at the fair. By 1870, Baldwin had become the largest producer of locomotives in the

United States. The founder of the company, Matthias W. Baldwin, was a staunch Presbyterian, an abolitionist, and a close political supporter of Thaddeus Stevens, the abolitionist Congressman who joined Bingham in conveying the articles of impeachment to the Senate in Johnson's trial.[11] Baldwin had passed away by the time Bingham had been assigned to serve in Japan. But another important industrialist from Bingham's hometown neighborhood was quite active. Henry Kirke Porter, Chairman of H.K. Porter Works, had studied theology as a young man and followed politics closely. Bingham's persistence and Porter's railway equipment were finally able to break the British stranglehold on the Japanese market. [12]

Five years after the Philadelphia Centennial, Bingham was able to tell Secretary Evarts that America had successfully completed a railway in Hokkaido that was longer than the Bristish-built line from Yokohama to Tokyo. It also boasted all American cars and equipment. The Minister further bragged that the line was completed at one eighth the price per mile of the shorter British railway.[13] Bingham may have overstated the comparison, but his enthusiasm for poking the British in their commercial eye was pure and sincere. The success of Baldwin Locomotive Works followed. By the end of the century, Baldwin had "exported more locomotives to Japan than any other foreign manufacturer by far." [14] Bingham understood that changing the rules that governed trade policy was crucial. But in the meantime, there was business to be done. And Bingham's Legation played an important role in doing just that.

Team gathered for inaugural of Poronai Railroad in Hokkaido. The tall man on the right with the hat is Joseph Crawford of the Pennsylvania Railroad who supervised construction of the first American railway in Japan. Archives of the Japanese Railway Museum, Omiya.

Logo of H. K. Porter Co. of Pittsburgh, PA on body of the engines supplied to the Poronai Railroad. Photograph by author.

173

H. K. Porter locomotive on the track in Hokkaido.
Archives of the Japanese Railway Museum, Omiya.

CHAPTER EIGHTEEN
Success, Delay and the Next Generation

Tokyo – During Minister Bingham's final years in Tokyo, his legacy was secure. Japan was at peace internally and with its Pacific neighbors. His major policy goals had either been won or were advancing toward a positive outcome. The Legation was well-housed, and plans for a new site were underway. The mission was well-managed, and a new generation, mentored by Bingham, was taking positions of importance in the Japanese and American bureaucracies. The United States diplomatic presence in Japan was secure, and its reputation respected. In short, John Bingham had accomplished a lot in his twelve years as minister.

Revision of America's unequal treaty with Japan continued to move forward but was not finally resolved during Bingham's term. Within the international diplomatic community, Bingham had played a major role in bringing about treaty revision. Alone within the diplomatic community during his first years in Japan, Bingham faced criticism from the press and indifference in Washington. Japan, once again, proposed another multilateral conference, this time for the summer of 1884. In Washington, the German Legation had convinced the State Department that the Japanese had a proposal that should help move the stalled treaty revision process forward. But when the Japanese proposal was brought to the table, the process stalled.[1]

Once the conference disbanded, it was not until May of 1886, after Bingham's retirement, that the issue was once again formally considered. In 1888, both the United States and German ministers in Tokyo agreed on a text. Regrettably, once in the hands of the State Department in Washington, the American text was held up and was never submitted to the Senate for consideration and approval. One concern was that the provision allowing for reciprocal ownership of land by aliens of the two countries would make Senate approval unlikely.[2] Some Americans feared the prospect of American land being bought up by immigrants from across the Pacific. Anti-Asian political sentiment had grown along with expanded white American settlement on the West Coast. Race had begun to obscure the missionary/academic lobbying lens through which many in Washington had viewed Asia.[3]

In the Spring of 1883, Bingham was thrilled to receive a message from Secretary of State Frelinghuysen informing him that Congress had voted to return the $785,000.87[4] indemnity payment that had been forced on the Tokugawa government decades earlier. Deeply involved in the politics of repayment and aligned with political forces back home which favored this move, Bingham had been confident that the issue would be settled. It had only been a matter of when. In a reply to the Secretary dated April 30, Bingham said that he would be handing over the payment to the Minister of Foreign Affairs Inouye Kaoru in person.[5] Resolution of the indemnity issue was a success Bingham could claim.

Washington, D.C. - As 1884 was drawing to a close, Democrat Grover Cleveland's election was expected to bring change in the

Legation's leadership, A loyal Republican, Bingham had supported James G. Blaine, former Senator and briefly Bingham's superior as Garfield's secretary of state. In an election where the issue of corruption in government was paramount, Blaine was tainted by scandal and Cleveland portrayed as an enemy of corruption. Blaine won in Ohio, but despite a scandal involving fathering a child out of wedlock, Cleveland won a close election.

In the run up to the election, Bingham did not escape partisan attempts to paint him as corrupt. Attacked in both House and Senate, Bingham was accused of misuse of funds in the initial arrangements in setting up the Legation in Tsukiji in 1874. Sympathetic Congressman Robert R. Hitt, of Illinois detailed the charges in a long letter to the minister.[6] Hitt had served as a diplomat in Paris during the Grant administration and as Assistant Secretary of State under Garfield and part of the Arthur administration. He knew Congress and he understood Washington politicking surrounding State Department budgets. When the issue had first come up, during the campaign to associate the State Department with the corruption attributed to Blaine, Bingham had replied with detailed information on the transactions a decade earlier.[7] As far as the possibility for continuing his assignment in Tokyo, Hitt wrote that the Democrats are "very hungry and very thirsty."[8]

Tokyo - Settlement of the Shimonoseki issue led to an offer from Japan that would allow the minister to add another success. At the end of 1884, Foreign Minister Inoyue contacted Bingham to get his assessment of what the change in parties in the White House might mean for the bilateral relationship. Inoyue also expressed gratitude for the indemnity reversion and informed Bingham that to show its gratitude, the Meiji government was prepared to make a gift of land in *Akasaka* worth $25,000 for a new Legation site.[9] In reporting this to Frelinghuysen, Bingham advised quick acceptance of Japan's offer and requested $40,000 for construction of a new Legation.[10] The secretary passed the message to President Arthur who concurred. Arthur directed the Secretary to also pass the message along to Congress with a budgetary request. In the lame duck Congressional session, the issue was not taken up and no agreement was concluded before Bingham left Japan. But his legacy in the mission's physical plant still stands; the current Embassy and the Ambassador's residence stand on the Akasaka site.

Bingham's successor, former Texas governor Richard Hubbard, was satisfied with the Legation's Tsukiji location. Without pressure from the mission in Tokyo, the move to new quarters languished until 1889, when the landlord of the Tsukiji property forced a decision. The property the Legation had occupied since the beginning of Bingham's term was being sold to make room for a club. There was no longer a choice. The newly-arrived minister who came to Japan in 1889, John Franklin Swift, oversaw the final move to Akasaka. Swift wrote Bingham asking for a photograph of the former minister and for help in rounding up similar photographs from the other former chiefs of mission. Swift also reassured Bingham that the library the Ohioan had so lovingly built up at the Tsukiji location would be transferred to the new site.[11] Although the books stayed in Tokyo, Bingham carefully brought with him receipts on the transactions when the Legation was first set up in Tsukiji. If the charges of corruption that had erupted against him were to come up again, Bingham, as usual, would be ready with the details.

Even before leaving Cadiz for Tokyo in 1873, John Bingham had begun to establish a cadre of Americans whose role in the bilateral relationship continued to be critical well into the 20th century. Traveling with the Bingham family on their first trip across the Pacific, Durham Stevens remained at the Legation as deputy for a decade. Entering service with the Imperial Government in 1883, he first joined the Japanese Legation in Washington and worked on the treaty issue from there. Assigned again to Tokyo, he joined Count Inouye on a mission to Korea to negotiate the settlement of Japanese claims against Korea. The claims had arisen from destruction of the Japanese Legation and loss of Japanese lives during the 1884 coup which pitted pro-Meiji Korean forces against those favoring Korean ties to the Chinese Empire. From 1885 to 1887, Stevens again spent most of his time in Tokyo, this time as a member of the Japanese team working on revision of the unequal treaties.

In Bingham's later years in Tokyo, Henry Denison was also involved in treaty revision issues as an advisor to the Japanese Ministry of Foreign Affairs. There he forged a close working relationship with young Japanese ministry officials. His relationship with Shidehara Kijuro was to become important in the coming years. By the end of the 1880s, Denison's wife had become ill and no longer lived with her husband in Japan. Until his death in 1914, he lived a discreet personal life as a bachelor in Tokyo. He participated with equal discretion as a member of Japan's team at the negotiations that ended both the Sino-Japanese War and the Russo-Japanese War. Denison was also praised for his behind-the-scenes work in helping negotiate the Anglo-Japanese Alliance of 1902.[12]

The Treaty of Portsmouth[13], agreed upon by Russia and Japan in 1905, was a key event in the lives of both Stevens and Denison. Japanese leaders were confident that in Korea, Japan had a "manifest duty...to provide that country with a stable government, under which they may enjoy tranquility and the prosperity which follows in its train."[14] Japan's absorption of Korea as a protectorate ignited Korean nationalism. Assigned back to Washington as honorary counsellor, Stevens assisted Japan's treaty negotiations with Mexico. He was also twice sent to Hawaii to help settle claims of Japanese subjects for losses from a bubonic plague epidemic.[15]

In 1904, Stevens was appointed to the Korean Foreign Office. On leave to visit family in the United States in March, 1908, Stevens was shot by a Korean assassin in San Francisco as he prepared to cross the bay to take the train to Washington. He made the trip in a casket. At his funeral in Washington, D.C., Secretary of State Elihu Root served as one of the pallbearers. In a letter to an American naval officer warning how poisonous immigration restrictions would be to Japanese and American relations written just months before his death, Stevens declared that the "unselfish friendship by the United States for this [Japan] the most progressive and receptive among the nations of the East" that had been nurtured by Perry, Harris and Bingham, was vital for America and for Asia.[16] Stevens is fondly remembered in Japan. He is a pariah in Korea. He is all but forgotten among his own countrymen.

As we have seen, Henry Denison was a trusted member of the Japanese delegation at Portsmouth, in the talks that ended the Russo-Japanese War. During his years as an advisor to the Meiji Government Denison took and preserved detailed notes. His records for the critical years of 1905-10 are not among his documents left behind when he died. Shidehara, the foreign service officer who had been a close friend of Denison for years, was convinced Denison destroyed the papers to make certain there was no evidence that would lessen perceptions of Foreign Minister Baron *Komura Jutaro's* contribution in concluding the Treaty of Portsmouth.[17] A bust of Henry Denison is displayed at the Diplomatic Training Center in *Sagami Ono*, west of Tokyo. It is a unique honor for an American employed by Japan's Ministry of Foreign Affairs.

Shidehara continued for years to play a major part in the bilateral relationship. As Foreign Minister, he represented the Japanese government at the cornerstone laying of the Ambassador's residence in 1929.[18] The Residence still stands on the site where Bingham knew it would be one day. Denison's friend also played another significant role, when as Prime Minister during the years of the American military

*Bust of Henry Denison at the Ministry of Foreign Affairs
Training Center in Sagami Ono. Photo by author.*

181

occupation, he had a two-hour private conversation with General Douglas MacArthur. During their talk, Shidehara is credited with convincing MacArthur to keep the Emperor on the Chrysanthemum Throne.[19]

When an additional position for an American officer at the Legation was finally approved in the last years of Bingham's tenure, he asked Edwin Dun to fill the slot. Almost a decade earlier, Bingham had assisted Dun with legal formalities for Dun's marriage to his Japanese wife. Although a Democrat, Dun was from Ohio, and the two shared a respect for Japan, its politics and culture. Ready to relocate from Hokkaido where he was working, Dun and his family were pleased to be in Tokyo. After Bingham's departure for Cadiz, the two continued to correspond. Dun went on to become Legation secretary and then minister from 1893-1897. In those positions, he continued to push for treaty revision and on the Legation property issue, following the policy path first laid out by Bingham. Upon the death in 1891 of Yoshida Kiyonari, former Japanese Minister to Washington during Bingham's Japan years, Dun sent Bingham a letter which recognized Bingham's closeness to Yoshida and contained a heartfelt endorsement by Dun for all he had learned while working with the elder Ohioan.[20] After leaving his position as Minister, Dun remained in Japan as representative for Standard Oil and is buried with family members in Aoyama cemetery in Tokyo.

With his time in Tokyo drawing to a close, the curtain had not yet shut on the melodrama with Consul General Van Buren. Working in Washington in 1883, Stevens was able to update his former superior about Van Buren's efforts in Washington. In early 1883, Stevens reported to Bingham that Van Buren had met with Secretary of State Frelinghuysen and that the consul general had spoken badly of the

Edwin Dun and family. He is pictured with Yama, his second wife, and their four sons. Hokkaido University Library Archives.

minister.[21] Like Van Buren, Frelinghuysen was from New Jersey and it was awkward for him to confront the consul general's hometown supporters. Van Buren did try to repair his reputation, becoming active in the Asiatic Society, whose members were typically academic types. In fact, he published two useful but prosaic reports, "Labor in Japan" and "Porcelain in Japan". The reports were a collection of information typical of consular reports to Washington, bound into a small journal with the consul general's name on the title page.[22]

Van Buren continued to get into scrapes. In 1882, the consul general had gotten into a spat with the *Japan Weekly Mail* which he felt had slandered him.[23] Then in 1884, his last year in Yokohama, Van Buren became embroiled in his final and perhaps noisiest public altercation in the community. He sued his rival for election to the presidency of the Yokohama United Club for slander, claiming $5,000 in damages. Since the case involved the consul general who normally sat as judge in the American consular court in Yokohama, Bingham, as Van Buren's superior, was required to take the bench. The minister's judgement found against his consul general. The *Gazette* and the *Herald*, eager for gossipy controversy, noisily took opposing sides.[24] Bingham's voluminous judgement went on for pages as Bingham channeled his frustration into exhaustive legal prose, a medium he may have found therapeutic.

When they returned from home leave in 1879, John and Amanda were pleased to have their grandchildren with them, but the young voices did not drown out the family's adult problems. Daughter Lucy's widower, Samuel Frazier, had returned to Japan along with his children, and had taken an academic job in Tokyo. Then in 1881, David Thompson decided to leave his position as legation interpreter to devote himself full time to his missionary calling. When Bingham made the controversial decision to give the interpreter job to Frazier, he was attacked for nepotism in the local English language press. An anonymous letter in the *Japan Mail* complained that with the Frazier case, along with Bingham's securing of the Japanese Legation job in Washington for Stevens, the minister had "drawn a straight flush."[25] A follow up reply-letter[26] by an anonymous supporter defended Bingham's action, explaining that there was only one qualified candidate and that that individual had refused the position.

By February, 1883, Frazier was on a ship returning to the States. Bingham forwarded a note through the insurance company to make sure someone from Frazier's family met him when he arrived in San Francisco. Bingham's letter to Frazier's father said that his "infirmities" necessitated Frazier's resignation from the interpreter's position. But the suddenness of the departure and Bingham's turning over of all responsibility for Frazier's well-being to Frazier's relatives in the United States, while his two children remained in Tokyo, hinted at a strain in Frazier's relationship with the Binghams.[27] Within a year of his departure from Japan, Samuel Frazier was healthy enough to remarry and took up a pastorate in Youngstown, Ohio. By the summer of 1885, Frazier was robust enough to give a well-received talk about his experience in Japan at Chautauqua, a summer gathering of scholars, thinkers, and religious leaders that continues even today in upstate New York.

Texas - Daughter Marie and her toddler son, Robert, also returned to Tokyo with John and Amanda. The minister searched for a way to bring the family together. To do that, it was necessary to have the Army agree to release Major Wasson from his duties as Army paymaster in west Texas. Wasson could then come to Tokyo. Curtailing his military assignment required Congressional approval. In Japan, he would need a job, and Bingham was in a position to make both happen. On December 27, 1882, the House of Representatives considered a motion to release Wasson from his payroll duties in Texas to allow him to take up a position as advisor to the chief survey officer of the Japanese Home Ministry.[28] Had he returned to Tokyo, Wasson may have faced additional problems. The dashing officer had been gone from Japan for three years, but the gambling debts he had left behind were neither forgiven nor forgotten. A scandal that broke the next year kept him in the United States.[29]

In early 1883, seeking to pay off a poker debt of $5,500, more than twice his annual pay of $2,500, Wasson staged a fake robbery of the army payroll in Texas. By the summer, he had been arrested, tried, convicted, and sent to the military prison at Ft. Leavenworth, Kansas. The embarrassment for Bingham was acute but not intense enough to deter the minister from writing to former President Grant to appeal Wasson's case. Grant declined to intervene with President Arthur. By the end of 1884, Wasson has been released from prison and had begun a long period of rehabilitation. In both the Frazier and Wasson cases, complaints in the English language press were noisy and the minister was criticized by his opponents for favoritism but no formal charges were brought against the minister.

In February, 1883, Bingham moved quickly to fill the vacancy for a Legation staff interpreter left by Frazier's embarrassing departure. He hired family friend Willis N. Whitney. The Whitney family were members of the Tokyo Union Church and Willis Whitney's mother and Amanda Bingham were good friends.[30] Dr. Whitney had spent years of his adolescence in Japan while his father pursued a fitful career as a teacher of business. His sister's diary is a motherlode of intimate details of family life of the American community in Tokyo in those years.[31] Encouraged by Hepburn and Bingham, Whitney had entered the University of Pennsylvania, where he earned a medical degree before returning to Japan to practice. The first Legation American employee to have grown up in Japan, Whitney continued as interpreter until the summer of 1895 when Edwin Dun began serving as Minister.

When Sir Harry Parkes left Japan in 1883 to become Her Majesty's Minister to China, Bingham once more took on the role of dean of the diplomatic corps. With the opening of the *Rokumeikan* or Deer Cry Pavilion, an entertainment center with Gilded Age pretentions, the Binghams now headed the list for any formal diplomatic occasion. There were fancy dress balls like one in November 1884, celebrating Emperor Meiji's birthday.[32] And there were smaller social gatherings, dinners with Prime Minister Ito Hirobumi and his wife and Foreign Minister Inoyue Kaoru and his spouse which also included daughters Emma and Marie. The elite of the foreign community had frequent social interaction with the highest levels of Japan's political world. Bingham gave little indication that he relished such events.

For Bingham personally, the Union Church in Tsukiji, where his wife Amanda was active, continued to be an anchor and a refuge from the internecine distractions of life in Japan's small foreign community. During his time in Japan, Protestantism continued to attract new believers, but by the time he left to return to Ohio, there were only slightly more than ten thousand Japanese converts. Given the fact that there were 138 American missionaries in Japan in 1883, and that missionaries from other countries were also active, the ratio of souls saved to soul savers was disappointing.[33] The stern Calvinism of Bingham and many of his co-religionists continued to be an important conduit for transmission of western culture to Japan. And although Protestant Christianity had established a firm foothold in Japan, the footprint was small and not growing quickly.[34]

In a farewell message just after Cleveland's inauguration, Frelinghuysen wrote that he hoped Cleveland would keep America's "efficient representative" in Japan.[35] Frelinghuysen's comments might imply that Bingham had a desire to remain. Desire perhaps. Expectation, certainly not. John and Amanda agreed, it was time to return to Ohio.

CONCLUSION

From Menace and Mastery to Sympathy and Persuasion

Were we asked to sum up the results of Judge Bingham's official doings in Japan, we should place first the fact, that he has taught the Japanese the possibility of making a friend of a foreign minister. That signifies a great deal. It signifies that there has been a change for which thoughtful Westerners in China also are beginning to be impatient – the substitution of sympathy and persuasion for menace and mastery. That it has been a substitution beneficial to the material interests of Americans themselves, is sufficiently proved when we observe that to be a citizen of the United States has become a passport to the confidence and liking of the Japanese...it is nevertheless certain that his undeviating integrity, large charity, and fine intellect have imparted to his official career in Japan the dignity of a standard, by which the better classes of his countrymen will involuntarily measure their future representatives. And it is equally certain he has earned for the United States in this part of the Orient a reputation never before enjoyed by any Western Power in the East.[1]

Editorial in *Japan Weekly Mail*, July 18, 1885.

John Bingham exerted more influence on the bilateral relationship between Japan and the United States during the Meiji Period than any other American. From the beginning and during much of his tenure in Japan, Bingham and the policies he espoused had been excoriated in the English language press, noisy broadsheets that were mostly beholden to British interests.[2] But, when he left, the British owned and operated *Japan Mail*, as well as the Japanese *JiJi Press*, expressed deep respect for his integrity and intelligence. His vital contribution to the development of Japan and enhancement of American influence in the region were broadly recognized and finally appreciated.

Bingham's generation and the generation that followed him, both in America and Japan, recognized his important contributions to American diplomacy. In a book published in 1903, former Secretary of State, John Watson Foster, praised Bingham's role in working to revise the unequal treaties with Japan.[3] And just months before he was killed, in a letter to a friend, Durham W. Stevens, by then an advisor to the Korean government, placed Bingham alongside Perry and Harris in displaying "…repeated proofs of unselfish friendship by the United States for this the most progressive and receptive among the nations of the East."[4]

But as the 20th century unfolded, that recognition faded. Bingham's years in Japan were no longer celebrated, but rather ignored. Shortly after his retirement and return to Cadiz, Bingham was approached to write an autobiography, one that would emphasize his interactions with Lincoln, Grant, Stanton and Custer. The publisher suggested "The whole could be written in such a way as to not be offensive to the Southern people where large sales would be made."[5] Bingham did not take up the offer. No further opportunities were forthcoming, and no champion of his legacy appeared.

A generation after Bingham's death, Walter Shotwell published a short piece about Bingham in a series of biographical sketches of political figures, entitled *Driftwood*. Shotwell was the son of a close personal friend of Bingham, and lamented that a biography of Bingham would likely never be written. To Shotwell, the reasons Bingham had become neglected were clear: his family and papers had scattered, his political colleagues had passed away, and there was no one in the small town of Cadiz to promote his memory. Of Bingham's years as a diplomat, which he described as a period of leisure for the minster, Shotwell wrote only that in Japan, Bingham "sat down to rest and, as it proved, to rust."[6] Bingham had been mostly forgotten and when remembered, belittled.

In recent years, there has been a revival of interest in Bingham, particularly his contribution to American constitutional history through the 14th Amendment. There is now an excellent biography[7] and a growing literature that examines the role Bingham played in that key addition to America's fundamental legal document.[8] But his years in Japan remain largely unexplored.

Shotwell's reasons are not wrong, but they are insufficient. Bingham had never been a self-promoter. Certainly, he had been politically ambitious. But he advocated for ideas and values, and disliked self-aggrandizement and ostentatiousness in others and in himself. In looking at the materials in the *Ronsheim Collection*, which gives insight into his character, it is telling to recall what kind of documents and materials he chose to keep. These were largely notes that held some personal or sentimental value or documentation that he felt he might need if a sensitive financial or personnel issue should reappear. There was little boasting about his considerable accomplishments.

If it were true, as Shotwell wrote, that his papers we scattered, it is also true that he made no effort, even in his early, healthy years of retirement, to construct or record a historical legacy. He did make an occasional speech and submit to several interviews. By contrast, Commodore Perry went on the speaking circuit and published enthusiastically about his exploit in opening Japan. Bingham, with years of insight into Japanese political culture, saw no need to broadcast his Japan experience. Similarly, he did little to claim credit for his contributions as a Congressman.

It is also true that his family did little to champion his legacy. The widow of fellow Cadizian, George Armstrong Custer, made it her life's mission to make certain her husband was not forgotten. The popularity of her book and lectures and the colorful events of Custer's life ensured this was so. Bingham's descendants did little to promote his memory. His sons-in-law both had unpaid notes due to Bingham when he died; they left debts rather than accolades. Surviving daughters Emma and Marie left Cadiz and lived out their lives in Montclair, New Jersey. Shotwell was correct. Like the papers, the family had scattered.

Bingham's reserve extended even to his decisions regarding his grave site. Thomas Van Buren, Bingham's nemesis in the Japan years, is buried just inside the main gate of a prominent cemetery in Englewood, New Jersey. The grave boasts an elaborate statue that towers over any visitor. John Bingham and wife Amanda have a modest headstone in a small-town cemetery. Bingham's funeral was not without pomp, and his grave is not undistinguished, but, like the man buried there, it is unostentatious. His Calvinist forbearers would have approved.

The footsteps of history also drowned out Bingham's legacy. Supreme Court cases in the last decades of the nineteenth century entrenched Jim Crow laws and all but obliterated Bingham's intended effect of the 14th Amendment. One hundred years later the revival of that amendment and the Civil Rights movement resuscitated interest in John Bingham among constitutional lawyers. On the 150th anniversary of the amendment's adoption in 2018, interest in Bingham among scholars of American constitutional law had become significant.[9]

In East Asia and in America's relationship to Japan, developments in the international diplomatic environment overtook Bingham's expectations for peace. Rather than serve as a benign model for economic development for the region, Japan joined the western powers in an escalating scramble for imperial position. At the time of Bingham's death there was still optimism, including among some Christian missionaries, that Japan could lead Korea along the path that Japan had taken with the Meiji Restoration. The assassination in 1908 of Bingham mentor Durham Stevens, who was serving the Japanese colonial administration in Korea, was dramatic evidence, as was the assassination the following year of Ito Hirobumi, that by the early twentieth century that path had been blocked by ethno-nationalism.

Just a year earlier, in the Gentlemen's Agreement of 1907, Japan had agreed not to send emigrants to the United States and the United States, in turn, promised not to enact laws to ban Japanese from immigrating. The expansive world view of Webster, Seward, and Bingham was collapsing inwardly from the forces of nationalism and racial identity. Bingham's confidence in America's providential role in history could easily depreciate into paternalism and degenerate into arrogance. But Bingham's career showed genuine respect for Japan and her citizens and he worked hard to realize a bilateral relationship of influence and cooperation, not domination and control.

In more recent times, Ambassador Mansfield was fond of calling America's relationship with Japan "the most important bilateral relationship in the world, bar none."[10] By 1885, as Bingham was leaving Tokyo, Japan and America had begun to assume the important joint role Ambassador Mansfield so often extolled. Great Britain's ascendency of international relations in Asia was no longer unchallenged. Japan was rapidly ingesting western technology and digesting western institutions. In a very short time, the Emperor's government had become a viable participant in Pacific political and military affairs.

America's forays across the Pacific in the years before the Civil War had been tentative. By 1885 America's commitment to a Pacific presence was firmly established. From Bingham's time until Mansfield's tenure and beyond, through periods of conflict or cooperation, there has been no relationship among Pacific powers that has consistently approached the importance, over time, of America's relationship with Japan. Always looming, and in recent decades emerging as a Pacific power, China is remaking the dynamics of diplomacy in East Asia. Still, the relationship between Japan and America is crucial. And it is helpful to remember how Bingham built the initial, critical institutional framework of that relationship.

When Bingham arrived, Japan was a diplomatic backwater; the American Legation was understaffed and poorly housed. When he left, Japan, through prodigious efforts of its leaders and people, had earned a place as a participant in the great power politics of East Asia. Under his tutelage, American diplomats had developed an important personal network with Japanese officials. And American prestige was well established, both within the corridors of the Meiji government and in the reception rooms of the other legations in Japan. Bingham was both a talented diplomat and a skilled manager whose influence on the bilateral relationship between Japan and America was profound and long-lasting. Just as importantly, through example and deportment, he set a tone for Japanese and American political and social interactions that was respectful. Bingham led by both effort and example.

Diplomacy is seldom effectively practiced by command. As Bingham knew well from years of experience shepherding delicate issues through the political maze on Capitol Hill, diplomacy demanded persuasion, cooperation, persistence and a long-term view of America's relationship to Japan and its role in the Pacific. The record is clear. John

Bingham was an outstanding diplomat. But over the years his record has faded with time and has been obscured by more dramatic but often less important events and personalities. Undoubtedly Bingham was the most important American figure in the bilateral relationship between the United States and Japan during a crucial period of dramatic, sometimes violent change in both societies. His contributions deserve far more recognition than they have received over the years.

APPENDIX
Consulates

In addition to the Legation in Tokyo and the Consulate General in Yokohama, Bingham oversaw consulates in Hakodate in Hokkaido, Nagasaki on the southern Japanese island of Kyushu, and at Hyogo (Kobe). Management control of the consulates was loose but Nagasaki and Kobe did have significant American communities.

Nagasaki - When Bingham arrived in Japan, Willie P. Magnum, from a prominent North Carolina political family, had been serving as Consul for eight years. Before being assigned to Nagasaki he had served in China. Nagasaki had a sizeable Chinese community and acted as a jumping off spot for travel to China from Japan. In 1881 Magnum was succeeded by Alexander Jones. Like many America consuls, Jones had served in the Civil War and had reached the rank of Brigadier General. Jones fought at the Battle of Allegheny Mountain and the Battle of Gaines Mill, during the Peninsula Campaign. He fought for the Confederacy. Jones' appointment was less unusual than it may seem. The Republicans needed political support in the South and appointment to government positions was one benefit the administration had to hand out.

Hyogo (Kobe) – The consul at Kobe, Julius Stahel, was also a Civil War general. Major General Stahel had been born in Hungary in 1825. He joined the Hungarian revolution in 1848, then immigrated to the United States just before the outbreak of the Civil War. He was present for both Battles of Bull Run, played an important role as a cavalry commander at Gettysburg and was in the audience when Lincoln gave his famous address at the dedication of the cemetery there. Before assignment to Hyogo, Stahel had served for several years as consul in Yokohama. During his world tour Grant became convinced that many American diplomats serving overseas were unqualified and too many were corrupt. Upon his return, he asked Secretary of State Evarts to create an inspection team to examine and root out these problems. Stahel was one of the officers chosen to investigate corruption within the Foreign Service in Asia and elsewhere.

Major General Julius Stahel, Medal of Honor recipient for bravery in leading his division into action at Piedmont, Virginia, 1864.

Consul in Kobe 1877-1884.

Consul General Shanghai 1884-1885.

Photograph from Library of Congress.

Index

Common names such as Tokyo, Hong Kong and Meiji which will be familiar to most non-Japanese readers are not italicized in the text and not included on the above list. When a name is initially introduced it is italicized but in plain text thereafter. A few of the Japanese terms than have become commonly used but may not be familiar to many readers continue to be italicized throughout the text. Romanization is a rendering of the place or personal name in the language of that term. The pronunciations of the Chinese characters differ in Chinese, Korean and Japanese.

FOOTNOTES

Introduction

1 In Bingham's time in Japan the senior diplomat was the minister and the mission the legation. The terms ambassador and embassy came in to use in the early 20th century.
2 Gerard Magliocca, "The Father of the 14th Amendment", *New York Times*, September 17, 2013.
3 Hammersmith, *Spoilsmen.*

Chapter One

1 Like several other new Pennsylvania counties inaugurated that year, Mercer County was named for a hero of the Revolutionary War. Other Pennsylvania counties formed in 1800 and named for Revolutionary Military leaders were: Armstrong (Major General John Armstrong), Butler (General Richard Butler), Warren (Major General Joseph Warren) and Wayne (General Anthony Wayne). John H. Long, editor. *Pennsylvania Atlas of Historical County Boundaries.* Copyright, Newberry Library, 2008.
2 Felder, Paula S. "Hugh Mercer: An Unexpected Life." *Free-Lance Star*, Fredericksburg, VA, September 4, 2004. See also: https://web.archive.org/web/20050516210156/http://www.freelancestar.com/News/FLS/2004/092004/09042004/1488210_From a family of Presbyterian ministers, Mercer had come to Virginia from Scotland as a young man where he practiced medicine. Joining the fight for independence, Mercer was wounded and died at the Battle of Princeton in 1777.
3 The home where John Bingham was born still stands on the court house square in Mercer. It is now headquarters of the Mercer County Republican Party.
4 *History of Mercer County*, p. 363. Weekly postal service along the road from Pittsburgh in the south to Erie, Pennsylvania in the north passing through Mercer had opened just before Thomas Bingham had become postmaster. The road, at least in part, became known as Perry Highway and parts of the route maintain that designation even now.
5 *History of Mercer County*, p. 363.
6 *History of Mercer County*, p. 174.

7 Mercer County Republican Party website.

8 Jeremiah Evarts, father of William Evarts, served as Treasurer of the ABCFM from 1812-20 and as Secretary from 1821-31. He was father of Secretary of State William Evarts, appointed by President Rutherford B. Hayes and Bingham's principal for several years when he served as minister in Japan.

9 *Annual Report of the American Bible Society*, 1820, p. 22.

10 *Missionary Herald*, volume 23, 1827.

11 Wiley, "Lafayette in Western Pennsylvania."

12 Japan's Tokugawa government had been in power since 1603. The Tokugawa family ruled Japan through military control of a system of local lords and severely limited foreign contacts.

13 Hanna, *Historical Collections of Harrison County*, p. 197. This judicial position does not necessarily mean that Thomas Bingham had been admitted to the bar. See explanation on contemporary Ohio judicial system in Aynes, *Catholic Law Review*, pp. 881, 894 note 106.

14 Two ministers active in the Cadiz area during those formative years both figured in John Bingham's later life. The Reverend John Rae of the Associate Reformed Church was the grandfather of David Thompson, one of Bingham's closest associates in Japan. The Reverend John Walker of the more austere Associate Presbyterian Church and a strong anti-slavery advocate, was a dominating intellectual influence during Bingham's college years. Both Rae and Walker had studied at a newly established seminary in Canonsburg, Pennsylvania, Jefferson College. That modest seminary has grown into what is now Washington and Jefferson University in Washington, Pennsylvania. See Hanna, *Historical Collections of Harrison County*, p. 197 and Washington and Jefferson University website. There were distinctions between the Presbyterian groups in Mercer and Cadiz. Tait's Presbyterian Church in the United States of America was firmly established in a network of Presbyterian churches in the rest of the country and accommodated a wider range of views. The Associate Presbyterian Church to which John Walker adhered had a much stronger anti-slavery stance.

15 Aynes, "The Continuing Importance of Congressman John A. Bingham", p. 593. Richard Aynes, retired Dean Emeritus of the Akron University School of Law is the doyen of Bingham constitutional scholars. His detailed knowledge of Bingham's life and career is formidable. And his writings in prestigious legal

journals provide the backbone of a growing and increasingly visible body of scholarship on Bingham and his contributions to American constitutional history.

16 Aynes, "The Antislavery and Abolitionist Background of John A. Bingham", p. 890.

17 Beauregard, *Bingham of the Hills*, p. 5.

18 *History of Mercer County*, p. 287

19 *History of Mercer County*, p. 237. The date for William F. Clark's purchase of the *Luminary* is listed as 1833 but Aynes, "Antislavery and Abolitionist Background" p. 890 indicates 1831.

20 Beauregard, *Walker*, p. 96.

21 Beauregard, *Walker*, pp. 69-70.

22 Aynes, "The Antislavery and Abolitionist Background of John A. Bingham", pp. 910-1.

23 From website of the Native Hawaiian Bar Association, Honolulu, Hawaii.

24 Magliocca, p. 19.

25 Shotwell, *Driftwood*, p. 182.

26 Shotwell, pp. 183-4.

27 Shotwell, p. 182.

28 Beauregard, *Bingham of the Hills*, p. 10.

29 *History of Tuscarawas County*, p.366.

30 Magliocca, *American Founding Son*, p. 30.

Chapter Two

1 Magliocca, p. 37.

2 Magliocca, p. 35. This King James Version quote from Act 17: 26 also appears in comments Dr. James Hepburn is said to have made when he first landed at Batavia, now Java in Indonesia, in 1839. Hepburn, who created the first Japanese to English dictionary and was one of the first Protestant missionaries to arrive in Japan after the first treaty ports were opened was a colleague of Bingham in Japan. Overwhelmed by the color and cacophony of the Asian port, Hepburn wrote that God had made humanity of "one blood."

3 Magliocca, p. 40. Although called the Anti-Nebraska Party, the Convention that year is regarded as the founding of the Ohio Republican Party.

4 Beauregard, *Bingham of the Hills*, p. 23. Bingham received just

over sixty-three percent of the votes.

5 Magliocca, p. 39.

6 Curtis, "John A. Bingham and the Story of American Liberty", p. 628.

7 Beauregard, *Bingham of the Hills*, pp. 36-7.

8 Aynes, "The Antislavery and Abolitionist Background...", p. 917.

9 Beauregard, *Bingham of the Hills*, p. 42.

10 Zeitlow, "Congressional Enforcement of Civil Rights...", p. 727.

11 Beauregard, *Bingham of the Hills*, p. 52.

12 Speech by John Bingham in the House of Representatives, April 24, 1860. Printed as a pamphlet by the Republican Executive Congressional Committee and sold for $.50 for 100 copies.

13 Bingham's recollections reprinted in *Harrison*, p. 10.

14 Magliocca, p. 83.

15 Beauregard, *Bingham of the Hills*, p. 72-3, Magliocca, p. 83.

16 Marvel, *Lincoln's Autocrat – The Life of Edwin Stanton*, p. 313.

17 Magliocca, p. 92. Also see Beauregard, "President Lincoln and Congressman Bingham". Before traveling to Washington, Bingham spoke at a memorial service for the assassinated president at the Methodist Episcopal Church in Cadiz and in his remarks quoted the powerful 1845 abolitionist poem by James Russell Lowell key lines of which are:

For Humanity sweeps onward: where to-day the martyr stands,
On the morrow, crouches Judas with the silver in his hands;
Far in front the cross stands ready and the crackling fagots burn,
While the hooting mob of yesterday in silent awe return
To glean up the scattered ashes into History's golden urn.

18 Marvel, p. 377.

19 Magliocca, p. 92.

20 Magliocca, p. 95.

21 Magliocca, p. 99.

22 Blight, "Slavery Did Not Die Honestly", *Atlantic*, October 15, 2015.

23 Epps, *Democracy Reborn*, p. 262.

24 Aynes, "The Continuing Importance of Congressman John A. Bingham", p. 589.

25 Donnelly, *Constitution Daily*, John Bingham: One of America's Forgotten Second Founders.

26 Li, "The 14th: A Civil War-era amendment...", cover story *ABA*

Journal, posted May 1, 2017.

27 Beauregard, *Bingham of the Hills*, p.130. Bingham's margin was 416 votes out of 27, 098 cast.

28 *Ronsheim Collection*, roll I, item 620, letter from a constituent dated April 22, 1871.

29 Beauregard, *Bingham of the Hills*, p. 142.

Chapter Three

1 *The Papers of Ulysses S. Grant*, Volume 23, item 117, p. 91.

2 Foster, *Diplomatic Memoirs Volume I*, p. 5. Foster's career was capped by service as Secretary of State under President Benjamin Harrison after having been Minister to Mexico, Spain and Russia. He was grandfather of Cold War Secretary of State John Foster Dulles (1953-1959).

3 *"If that doubled-bolted land Japan, is ever to become hospitable, it is the whale-ship alone to whom the credit will be done; for already she is on the threshold."* Ishmael writes as he embarks on the *Pequod's* voyage in Melville's *Moby Dick*.

4 Hiram Bingham returned to the United States after 20 years in Hawaii due to his wife's ill health. The Mission Board subsequently turned down Bingham's request to return to Hawaii. He then spent some years as a pastor of an African-American Church in Brooklyn, New York. Friction surrounding Bingham's involvement in politics in Hawaii and the cultural clash between his approach to his mission and native Hawaiian customs was an open controversy. That John Bingham shared a surname made it certain he was aware of this other colorful Bingham. Anderson, Gerald H., editor. *Biographical Dictionary of Christian Missionaries*. William B. Eerdemans Publishing: Grand Rapids, MI. Paperback edition 1999.

5 Shewmaker, "Forging the Great Chain", p. 252. Webster's policy is described by Webster expert, Kenneth Shewmaker as "anti-colonialist, anti-interventionist and anti-monopolist."

6 Excerpt from speech of Senator William H. Seward to the Senate on the admission of California, March 11, 1850.

7 Bush, Lewis, *77 Samurai*, pp. 158, 166, 205. Bush's book is a recount of the Japanese version by Hattori Itsuro.

8 Choshu domain in the western area of Japan's main island of Honshu, and Satsuma, a larger domain in the island of Kyushu

were two of the leading domains in establishing the Meiji government in 1868. Many of the early Meiji leaders were from these domains.

9 Huffman, James A., *Edward House: A Yankee in Meiji Japan*, Lanham, Maryland: Rowman and Littlefield Publisher, Inc., 2003. Huffman's book details the remarkable career in Japan of a journalist who was close to major figures of the era including Ulysses S. Grant and Mark Twain.

10 A media favorite were the stories about Charles Longfellow, son of poet Henry Wadsworth Longfellow, who managed to spend twenty months and a large amount of his father's money in Japan beginning early in 1871. When Charles returned to New England, he did his part in introducing Japanese culture to his generation, with particular interest shown to his tattoos which included a large carp covering much of his back. Nootbar, "Charles Longfellow's Twenty Months in Japan", *Oita Provincial College of the Arts and Culture Research Journal*, Volume 52, 2015.

11 Japanese proper nouns and other terms are italicized when they first appear. Subsequent appearances are in plain text. Chinese characters (in Japanese, *kanji.* can be found in Appendix Two.) which also includes several Chinese and Korean words written in Chinese. A few Romanized Japanese terms that continue to be used in many English language sources are italicized throughout this text.

12 Mayo, "A Catechism of Western Diplomacy", pp. 389-410.

13 *Ronsheim Collection*, roll I, item 727.

14 John Bingham hired David Thompson as Legation interpreter shortly after he arrived in Japan. In 2013, retired Presbyterian missionary Sue Althouse began a series of articles on the website of the Presbyterian Historical Society about David Thompson and his wife, Mary Parkes Thompson. Mary came to Japan as a single woman missionary in 1872 and married David in Japan. Raised in Ashland County, Ohio, Mary was educated at Xenia Female Seminary in Xenia, Ohio. David died in Tokyo in 1915 and Mary remained in Japan until her death in 1927. For over 50 years, Mary kept a diary which along with other materials collected as the Thompson Papers, is in the archives of the Presbyterian Historical Society in Philadelphia. Mary's diary is the primary source for Sue Althouse's series of articles on the Thompsons.

15 Notehelfer, *American Samurai*, p. 15.

16 Notehelfer, various. Rather than continue reading law, Janes applied to enter West Point. During the Civil War, Lieutenant and then Captain Janes had a career that in summary seems unremarkable but which included experiences that apparently caused him not only physical but serious emotional damage. This included a religious experience that turned him from the more austere Free Presbyterian faith of his father to the more emotional religious sentiment of his mother. Leaving the Army, Janes retired to live on a farm in Maryland. In the meantime, the domain of Higo, modern Kumamoto Province, aware of the challenge faced from the West, was searching for a teacher for a school which was designed to introduce young samurai students to the outside world. Higo wanted a Christian and they wanted a soldier. Through a circuitous process that involved noted missionary Guido Verbeck, the Reverend John M. Ferris, Secretary of the Board of Foreign Missions of the Dutch Reformed Church, and Janes' father-in-law, Higo found and hired Captain L. L. Janes.

Once in Higo, with great energy and dedication, Captain Janes went about setting up his school and instructing the students, all in English. The training was rigorous and undoubtedly confusing for both students and teacher. But Janes' dedication was unquestionable and contagious.

17 Beauregard, *Bingham of the Hills*, p. 156.

18 *Ronsheim Collection*, roll I, item 727, letter from Eli T. Sheppard to John Bingham dated November 15, 1872. As soon as Sheppard knew that Bingham was not returning to the Congress he began a campaign to start his mentor off on his diplomatic career.

19 *Ronsheim Collection*, roll I, item 745, letter from Eli Sheppard to John Bingham dated December 2, 1872.

20 *Ronsheim Collection*, roll I, item 778, letter Eli Sheppard to John Bingham dated February 17, 1873.

Photo: Thompson with bureaucratic officials

1 Nakajima, "Diplomats and Missionaries", p. 54. Fourteen of the 19 student members of the delegation were from Saga. Later prominent Meiji era Christian politicians Kataoka Kenkichi of Kochi and Ebara Soroku of Shizuoka also joined the 38-member delegation.

Chapter Four

1 *Ronsheim Collection*, roll I, item 796.

2 *Ronsheim Collection*, roll I, item 810.

3 Pendleton, "William H. Lucas", Harrison County Historical Society website, April 3, 2010.

4 *Oberlin College Archives.*

5 *Morgan Library Collection*, Letter from E.L. Stevens to John Bingham dated May 13, 1856, in the Bingham Collection in the Morgan Library. The Morgan collection has two large boxes and one smaller box. The items are labeled but the labeling appears to be from an earlier organizing effort. The Morgan Library has held this collection since 1991.

6 *Ronsheim Collection*, roll I, items 812, 813.

7 *Japan Mail*, July 7, 1873.

8 Mitsubishi Corporation website section of company's origins with part on "Walsh Brothers". Walsh and Hall Company had begun in Nagasaki in 1862. By 1873 the American company had operations in Kobe and Yokohama as well. The Walsh brothers were active in sending Japanese to study in the States and often provided financial support. Their company had introduced mass manufacture of paper and they argued for a higher import tariff. When former Secretary of State Seward began his world tour with a visit to Japan, one of the Walsh brothers (it is unclear which) escorted Seward to his October visit to the Emperor. As a private citizen, Walsh did not proceed into the inner court and waited outside.

9 Murphy, *The American Merchant Experience in 19th Century Japan*, p.35.

10 Smith, *Ten Weeks in Japan*, p. 251.

11 Murphy, p. 83.

12 Seidensticker, p. 55.

13 The Reformed Protestant Dutch Church was incorporated in the United States in 1819. As it grew away from its European origins and services were more and more held in English. In 1867, the denomination changed its name to the Reformed Church in America. The church sent its first missionaries to Japan in 1859, including Guido Verbeck. See the website of the Reformed Church in America. https://www.rca.org/resources/rca-basics/brief-outline-rca-history

14 Jansen, *The Making of Modern Japan*, p. 355.

15 Ion, *American Missionaries, Christian Oyatoi*, p. 194.

16 Umetani, "The Role of Foreign Employees in Meiji…", p. 72.

Chapter Five

1 Beauregard, *Bingham of the Hills*, p. 150; *Ronsheim Papers*, Roll I, November 15, 1873.

2 Beauregard, *Bingham of the Hills*, p. 150. Beauregard notes that this quote is from the "Martin Collection". This source has not been confirmed by other research. However, the content of the letter reflects other statements about Japan and his mission there that Bingham made.

3 Yates, *Saigo Takamori: The Man Behind the Myth*, p. 130.

4 Eskildsen, "Transforming", p. 57.

5 Stephenson, "Charles LeGendre", *Dictionary of American Biography*, p. 146.

6 Iwata, *Okubo Toshimichi: The Bismark of Japan*, p. 191. Iwata writes that DeLong's involvement in the Korean invasion issue without Washington approval was the reason for his removal as minister.

7 Terashima's name is sometimes romanized as Terajima.

8 Iwata, *Okubo Toshimichi: The Bismark of Japan*. The choice of title for Iwata's book is instructive.

9 The Ryukyu Islands in Japanese were referred to as the Loo Choo Islands in the Chinese romanization of the period and as Liuqui in current romanization. Okinawa is the most prominent island in this long chain.

10 Eskildsen, "Of Civilization and Savages", p.418. Eskildsen argues that in looking for the roots of later Japanese imperialism in Asia, Japan's redefining of its national identity and international role from the 1870s was critical.

11 Mayo, "The Korean Crisis of 1873", p.793-6.

12 Daniels, p. 145, 147.

13 *FRUS*, Volume 1874-5, p. 678 quotes *Japan Daily Herald* article of April 7, 1874.

14 *Kaitakushi* was a Japanese project to develop the northernmost main island of Japan, Hokkaido. More about this project will be discussed later.

15 *FRUS*, Volume 1874-5, item 429, p. 675.

16 *FRUS*, Volume 1874-5, item 430, p. 681.

17 House, *The Japanese Expedition to Formosa*, p. 17.

18 House, p.21.

19 Huffman, p. 91.

20 *FRUS*, 1874-5, item 30, p. 155.

21 *FRUS*, 1874-5, item 31, p. 156.

22 Saigo Tsurumichi was the younger brother of Saigo Takamori, who remained in Kyushu. Saigo Takamori supported the incorporation of a contingent of 300 soldiers from Satsuma to join the expedition.

23 *FRUS*, Volume 1874-5, item 2, p. 764.

24 In the absence at post of the American Minister to China, the principal deputy chief of mission, in accordance with standard diplomatic procedure, had taken the title of Charge d'affaires ad inerim and assumed duties of the minister. I have seen no evidence that Williams and Bingham knew each other personally. But there is no doubt that they knew of each other. They shared a common overlapping network of political and missionary allies and contacts so certainly were well aware of each other's policies and intentions. Williams had first gone to China at age twenty-one to run the printing operations of the American Board of Commissioners for Foreign Missions. A staunch Presbyterian, Williams was a missionary for a time and in 1855 was appointed interpreter and secretary for the United States Legation to China. In 1853, he had joined Commodore Perry's mission to Japan as an interpreter

25 *FRUS*, Volume 1874-5, item 764, pp. 319-21.

26 Eskildsen, "Transforming," p. 253.

27 *FRUS*, Volume 1874-5, item 437, p. 688.

28 House, p. 225.

29 *FRUS*, enclosure 797 in China section of the document. Telegrams 78, 89, 117 between Henderson and Seward, August 5-7, 1874.

30 Beasley, *The Meiji Restoration*, p. 376.

31 *FRUS*, Volume 1874-5, item 439, p. 688.

32 *FRUS*, Volume 1874-5, item 443, p. 698.

33 LeGendre, Charles, *Progressive Japan*, C. Levy, New York, 1878.

34 *Japan Mail*, January 9, 1878.

35 LeGendre abandoned his New York socialite wife and married Ito Ikeda, illegitimate daughter of Matsudaira Yoshinaga, a well-known *bakumatsu daimyo*. The couple's son became a famous kabuki actor, Ichimura Uzaemon XV.

Chapter Six

1 Treat, Volume II, pp. 1-12.
2 Hammersmith, *Spoilsmen*, p. 48.
3 Treat, pp. 3-12.
4 Miscellaneous Documents of the House of Representatives, 1873.
5 Hall, *Mori Arinori*, pp. 198-9.
6 A petition to Congress listed colleges that were urging the use of the Shimonoseki Indemnity to fund education in Japan. The petition listed the following institutions:

Williams, Harvard, Vermont, Yale, California, Bowdin, Amherst, Bates, Bangor Theological Seminary, Union, Wesleyan, Middletown, CUNY, St. Lawrence, CCNY, State Normal School, Polytechnic and Collegiate Institute, Institute of Connecticut, Middlebury, Trinity, Burlington, University of Michigan, Northwestern, Hartsville, Beloit, Milton, Ripon, Carroll, Lafayette, Girard, Franklin and Marshall, Moravia College and Theological Seminary, Marietta, McKendree, Hamilton, State Normal School Westfield, State Normal School Trenton, Oxford Female Institute, Carleton, St. Joseph, Roanoke, Howard, Jonesborough Female College, Baylor, East Tennessee, Syracuse, Vassar, Columbia, Packer, Kalamazoo, Otterbein, Westminster Miscellaneous Documents of the House of Representatives for the third Session of the Forty-seventh Congress, 1872-3, Government Printing Office, 1873.

7 *Congressional Globe*, January 27, 1873, p. 891.
8 Pletcher, David, *The Diplomacy of Involvement*, p. 46. In addition to the destruction of the American whaling fleet the change from the use of lamps using whale oil to kerosene decimated the whaling industry.
9 Kahan, Paul, *The Presidency of Ulysses S. Grant*, p. 76.
10 The United States did not formally join the war with the French and the British but did participate in the treaty negotiations which followed. The terms of the treaty opened more and more of China to foreign commercial and religious penetration.
11 Sumner, *Complete Works*, volume 18, p. 96.
12 Ferris' name was to become quite familiar in Japan before the decade of the 1870s was out, when a school for women in Yokohama founded by female missionary Mary Kidder was named after him.
13 *Ministry of Foreign Affairs* (MOFA), Parkes letter to Terashima,

January 21, 1874, p. 462. (Japanese)

14 *FRUS*, Volume 1874-75, John Bingham to Hamilton Fish, November 18, 1873, item 413, p. 654.

15 *FRUS*, Volume 1874-75, John Bingham to Hamilton Fish, February 23, 1874, item 424, p. 669.

16 *FRUS*, Volume 1874-75, John Bingham to Hamilton Fish, January 19, 1875, #373, p. 753

17 Mayo, "A Catechism of Western Diplomacy", p. 389.

18 Murphy, Kevin C., *The American Merchant Experience in 19th Century Japan*, p. 85.

19 *FRUS*, Volume 1874-5, item 414, p. 655.

20 Mayo, "*Catechism*", p. 409.

21 *The Papers of Ulysses S. Grant*, Mississippi State University, Volume 24, 1873. In a series of messages dated January 21, February 23 and March 9, 1873, Bingham wrote to Grant explaining his view of the importance of treaty revision and complaining that Secretary of State Fish was unresponsive. Bingham requested Grant's intervention to prod Fish for a positive response. *The Papers* were first compiled in 31 volumes at the University of Southern Illinois, Carbondale: the collection has been digitized by the Mississippi State University, Starkville, Mississippi and resides in that collection.

22 White, *American Ulysses*, p. *504*.

23 Chernow, p. 826.

Chapter Seven

1 *FRUS*, Volume 1874-5, p. 645, Acting Secretary W. Hunter to Bingham, September 6, 1873.

2 *FRUS*, Volume 1874-4, item 412, page 654, Bingham to Fish, November 18, 1873.

3 *FRUS*, Volume 1874-5, item 416, p. 658. Fish to Bingham, January 7, 1874.

4 *FRUS*, Volume 1874-75, John Bingham to Hamilton Fish, November 19, 1874, item 365, p. 773.

5 Daniels, p. 143.

6 Satow, *A Diplomat in Japan*.

7 Dare, pp. 74-5. *Ronsheim*, roll 2 #979. In a private note to Bingham, Fish wrote that other diplomatic missions in Washington and London had heard that the Minister's statements

in Japan were being criticized and had put Sir Harry Parkes "in an awkward predicament."

8 *FRUS*, Volume 1876, December 7, 1875.
9 *FRUS*, Volume 1876, Fish to Bingham, April 5, 1876.
10 *Tokio Times*, January 7, 1877, p. 16.
11 *FRUS*, Volume 1874-5, item 411, p. 653.
12 *FRUS*, Volume 1876, item 191, Hamilton Fish to John Bingham, May 2, 1876.
13 Dare, p. 169.
14 Treat, *Early Diplomatic Relations Between the United States and Japan*, Volume II, pp. 8-10.

Chapter Eight

1 Hammersmith, *Spoilsmen*, p. 82.
2 *Tokio Times*, January 13, 1877. In January of 1877, journalist Edward House began publication of *Tokio Times*, a weekly newspaper. The *Times* took an American editorial point of view in an effort to balance the pro-British coverage of other papers. In his early editions, House wrote detailed accounts of the establishment of the various foreign missions in Japan. This information comes from the account on the American mission.
3 Although Bingham did not have the deep pockets of many diplomats, particularly those assigned to European postings, he was also certainly not indigent. His salary of $12,000 and rental properties back in the States provided a comfortable cushion during his years in Japan. Slightly above the salaries of a handful of the highest paid foreign experts hired by the Japanese, his means were clearly below those of some contemporaries in the expatriate community in Tokyo and Yokohama. This would include prominent business leaders and those with significant family resources back home like Consul General Van Buren and Daniel Crosby Greene, nephew of New York Senator and Hayes' Secretary of State William Evarts.
4 Hammersmith, p. 110; Dare, *John A. Bingham and Treaty Revision*, pp.57-58.
5 Fujita, *American Pioneers and the Japanese Frontier*, p. 3 and note p. 152. Fujita whose Japanese and English is impeccable and who has done major work on the topic of the *Kaitakushi* uses the term Hokkaido Development Department in English. Not a ministry,

the department was placed directly under the Council of State and was headed by a commissioner. The use of Hokkaido Development (or Colonization) Commission is also found.

6 Fujita, p. 10.

7 Fujita, p. 7.

8 Capron, *Memoirs*, pp. 281-9.

9 Capron, Memoirs, entry dated March 1, 1874. In his own diary, Capron records the transaction.

10 Hammersmith, p. 110.

11 Keene, *Emperor of Japan*, p. 207, Griffis, *Verbeck of Japan*, p. 255. Influential missionary, Guido Verbeck, who had arrived in Japan just after Dr. James Hepburn, had taken a position as advisor to the Meiji Department of Education in 1871. Verbeck is credited with influencing the Meiji government to send the Iwakura Mission.

12 Thompson, Mary, unpublished diary in the collection of the Presbyterian Historical Society, Philadelphia, Pennsylvania.

13 Mary Thompson's diary notes two agenda items from an April 6, 1874, meeting of the Presbytery and mission. First was acceptance of the resignation of Rothesay Miller. Miller, who was independently well off, had married Mary E. Kidder, sponsored by the Dutch Reformed Church, who had arrived in Japan in 1870. The Dutch Reformed Church had changed its name in 1869 to the Reformed church in America but the Dutch appellation was commonly used unofficially in the succeeding years. Living in Yokohama, Kidder established a school for girls which grew and is now Ferris University. Miller had changed denominational allegiance from Presbyterian to the Dutch Reformed Church in support of his wife's ministry. The change required the group's approval. The second agenda item was to determine whether it was permissible for Thompson to accept the interpreter position.

14 Dr. James Hepburn and Charles Carrothers both voted against Thompson's taking the interpreter position. They had also initially opposed the agreement by the Presbyterian, Congregational and Dutch Reformed denominations to join in a unified, "union" approach to their efforts in Japan. To these more conservative Presbyterians, denominational identity and distinction were very important.

15 Thompson, Mary. Diary entry December 31, 1874.

16 *Bible, 1st Corinthians xiv:40 (KJV) Let all things be done decently and in good order.*

17 *New York Times*, February 17, 1882, obituary for Joseph E.

218

Sheffield.

18 Statement of Citizens of Englewood, New Jersey, on the Removal of Thomas Van Buren from the Office of Commissioner General of the Vienna Exhibition, Hackensack, New Jersey, Daniel Drake Smith, Chairman, 1873.

19 *Ronsheim*, roll II, item 1030, Van Buren to Bingham, November 24, 1874.

20 *Ronsheim*, roll II, item 1031, Van Buren to Bingham, November 30, 1874.

21 *Ronsheim*, roll II, items 1032, 1033, 1036.

22 *Ronsheim*, roll II, item 1041, Van Buren to Henry Denison, February 15, 1875.

23 *Ronsheim*, roll II, also item 1041, Van Buren to Bingham, February 15, 1875.

24 *Ronsheim*, roll II, item 1042, Sheffield to Van Buren, February 15, 1875.

25 *Ronsheim*, roll II, item 1052, Van Buren to Bingham, June 29, 1875.

26 *Ronsheim*, roll II, item 1058, anonymous letter to Hamilton Fish, August 12, 1875.

27 *Ronsheim*, roll II, item 1064, Henry Denison to Bingham, November 3, 1875

28 *Morgan Library Collection*, Box 2, Van Buren to Bingham, March 8, 1876.

29 *Morgan Library Collection*, Box 2, Bingham to Van Buren, March 10, 1876. The fact that the correspondence on the Van Buren affair is so well preserved in the documents left behind at Bingham's death, suggests that he wanted a written record in the event of any further controversy.

Chapter Nine

1 Dickins, *The Life of Sir Harry Parkes: Minister Plenipotentiary to Japan*, Volume II, Macmillan and Co, London, 1894, quoting a series that appeared in *Japan Mail*, "Reports of Her Majesty's Secretaries of Embassy and Legations", 1873.

2 Jones, *Live Machines*, p. 109.

3 Dickins, quoting *Japan Mail*, see note 1 above.

4 Chamberlain, "In Memoriam, David Murray", from a collection of historical records of the State Street Presbyterian

Church, Albany, New York, held in Allen County Public Library. Chamberlain quotes Bingham's dinner speech of 1875.

5 Dare, p. 65.

6 *The Papers of Ulysses S. Grant*, Volume 22, January 26, 1872. *The Papers* were first compiled in 31 volumes at the University of Southern Illinois, Carbondale. The collection has been digitized by the Mississippi State University, Starkville, Mississippi, and resides in that collection.

7 Beauregard, "Samuel MaGill Bryan." After returning to Washington in 1884, Bryan became general manager of the Chesapeake and Potomac Telephone Company and died of cirrhosis of the liver at age 55, a wealthy man.

8 Ion, *American Missionaries*, p. 263.

9 Nish, *Iwakura Mission*, p. 100.

10 Griffis, *Verbeck of Japan*, p. 237. Verbeck's biographer quotes the European-born American missionary as saying, "Mine was a Smith and Wesson's revolver, bought, just before I left New Brunswick, by the advice of my Japanese friends."

11 Pieters, "Biography of James Ballagh", p. 106. Months before Bingham's arrival, Reformed Church missionary James H. Ballagh, on leave in the United States at the time, met with Secretary of State Hamilton Fish to ask for assistance in applying pressure on the Meiji government to release a Japanese convert from detention. If Bingham had not known Ballagh before, by the end of 1873 he knew him well. The access of a missionary to the Secretary of State is a testament to the influence this group exercised on American policy toward Japan in those years. Ballagh was an enthusiastic personality and had been in Japan since 1861. He is credited with performing the first baptism in Japan of a native Japanese in the Meiji era. He also had an important role in the formation of the so-called Yokohama Band, one of three early groups of Japanese Protestant Christians who became influential in the reintroduction of Christianity to Japanese society. With others, including David Thompson and Guido Verbeck, Ballagh was also instrumental in establishing a Japanese church that merged several important denominations including the American and Scottish Presbyterians and the Dutch Reformed Church into a single unified Japanese denomination, the United Christian Church of Japan.

12 Hialt, In this article posted on the internet, Hialt describes internal arguments in Japanese society and government for and

against cremation with tradition, sanitation and use of space all being areas of vigorous discussion and disagreement.

13 Hagin, *The Cross in Japan*, p. 169.

14 Althouse, Sue, "A Missionary Calling: A Day Causing Us to Pray Much", article on Presbyterian Historical Society website, March 4, 2016. Former missionary Sue Althouse has been organizing the Thompson papers and writing on Mary Thompson's Diary.

15 *FRUS*, Volume 1874-5, Hamilton Fish to John Bingham, September 20, 1875.

16 *Dun Reminiscences*, p. 30. Dun notes help from Bingham when he married. "After almost endless official requirements and red tape were complied with, the matter was finally arranged greatly through the good offices of Mr. Bingham, our minister."

17 *FRUS*, Volume 1876, John Bingham to Hamilton Fish, September 22, 1875. item180.

18 [18] *FRUS*, Volume 1874, John Bingham to Hamilton Fish, May 19, 1874.

19 *Ronsheim*, roll II, item 566, letter dated April 3, 1874

20 Capron, *Memoirs*. Capron's papers contained a letter from Bingham. Bingham wrote that although Capron had "been barked at by the small critics who control the English press in Japan," he would be remembered and revered by generations of Japanese to come for work that was honestly and wisely done.

21 *Ronsheim*, roll II, Capron to Bingham, May 17, 1875.

Chapter Ten

1 *Kudzu* vine, used for decorative and ground coverage purposes has become an invasive species throughout much of the American southeast.

2 "Characteristics of the International Fair", *Atlantic Monthly*, July, 1876, p. 90.

3 *Ronsheim*, Roll II, item 1111, Fish to Bingham. For a description of Hamilton Fish's personality, see Nevins, *Hamilton Fish, the Inner History of the Grant Administration*, in particular pp. 904-909.

4 *Helena Herald*, July 4, 1876.

5 http://www.ohiohistorycentral.org/w/Radical_Republicans.

6 *Hayes Library Manuscripts*, John Bingham to Rutherford B. Hayes, October 23, 1870.

7 *Ronsheim*, Roll II, item 1106, Rutherford B. Hayes to John Bingham, September 5, 1876.

8 *Ronsheim*, Roll II, item 1118, Eli Sheppard to John Bingham.

9 *Ronsheim*, Roll II, item 1116, Eli Sheppard to John Bingham, December 6, 1876.

10 *Ronsheim*, Roll II, item 1127, letter from D. Cunningham in Cadiz to Bingham, January 4, 1877.

11 Erastus Peshine Smith cut a flamboyant figure, indulging in both wine and women. Not all officials were pleased; there was also a sedate and decorous streak in many Japanese. Smith's outspoken castigation of the foreign community caused him to be ridiculed – he was labelled a "crapulous dotard" – in the English-language press. Smith also wore samurai dress with the traditional two swords, even though Japanese officials had already foregone them. After he departed Japan, the *Japan Weekly Mail*, August 26, 1876, wrote: "We have been informed by credible persons, that Mr. Peshine Smith showed some traces of ability of a certain kind, during such lucid intervals as confirmed habits of inebriety permitted him to enjoy."

12 *Ronsheim*, roll II, item 1091, Eli Sheppard to John Bingham, January 8, 1876.

13 *Ronsheim*, roll II, item 1096.10, Henry Denison to John Bingham, April 26, 1876.

14 *Ronsheim*, roll II, item 1089, E.L. Stevens to John Bingham, January 1, 1876. A copy of this letter is also in the *Morgan Library Collection*, Box 1.

15 Keene, p. 273.

16 *FRUS*, Volume 1878-79, p. 481, item 667, John Bingham letter to Secretary Evarts, November 13, 1877.

17 Maxfield, "The Legacy of Jeremiah Evarts," pp.172-5.

18 *Ronsheim*, roll II, item 1150, Frederick Seward to John Bingham, June 19, 1877.

19 Cunningham, p. 12.

Chapter Eleven

1 *FRUS*, Volume 1880-1881, p. 690/ item 438, John Bingham to William Evarts, July 24, 1880.

2 *Hayes Library Manuscripts*, letter from John Bingham to Rutherford B. Hayes, September 8, 1877.

3 Jones, *Extraterritoriality in Japan*, p. 128.

4 *FRUS*, Volume 1877, p. 636/ item 35, John Bingham to William Evarts, October 8, 1877.

5 *FRUS*, Volume 1877, item 199, John Bingham to William Evarts, May, 23, 1877.

6 FRUS, Volume 1877, item 597, p. 360, Bingham to Evarts, July 24, 1877.

7 Dare, p. 102.

8 Satow, p. 158.

9 *Japan Daily Herald*, July 28, 1877.

10 Jones, F.C., *Extraterritoriality in Japan*, p. 88.

11 *Tokio Times*, January 6, 1877. In his inaugural edition of a new English-language weekly published by journalist Edward H. House, the editor stakds out a strong position in favor of treaty revision. On the front page, House complained that, "It has long been obvious that the opinions of the present Secretary of State are guided in a direction which could not lead to entirely pleasant consequences."

12 Huffman, pp. 140-1.

13 Neuman, *America Encounters Japan.* p. 69. Article X was sometimes referred to as the "joker clause".

14 Treat, *Early Diplomatic Relations*, Volume II, p. 58 also quoted in Dare, p. 112.

Chapter Twelve

1 Whitney, *Clara's Diary*, p. 205.

2 *Hayes Library Manuscripts*, letter from John Bingham to Rutherford B. Hayes, October 10, 1877.

3 *Ronsheim*, roll II, Barton to John Bingham, May 22, 1878.

4 Campbell, *Citizen of a Wider Commonwealth*, p. 11.

5 *Ronsheim*, roll II, Yoshida to Bingham, September 21, 1876.

6 Keene, Emperor of Japan, p. 291.

7 *FRUS*, p. 821/ item 313, John Bingham to William Evarts, June 29, 1878.

8 *FRUS*, p. 807/item 311, John Bingham to William Evarts, May 16, 1878.

9 For an excellent and comprehensive treatment of this thesis, see Blight, *Race and Reunion.*

Chapter Thirteen

1 *Ronsheim*, roll II, Yoshida to Bingham, September 21, 1876.

2 Young, *Around the World with General Grant*, Volume II, p. 502.

3 Young, Around the World with General Grant, Volume II, p. 529

4 Chang, "General Grant's 1879 visit to Japan", pp. 385-7.

5 Campbell, p. 154.

6 McCartee, biographic entry, *Alumni Register of the University of Pennsylvania*, Volume V, p. 78.

7 *Grant Papers*, Volume 29, pp. 244-5.

8 Keene, *Emperor*, p. 315.

9 Campbell, p.167; *Grant Papers*, Volume 29, pp. 214-5.

10 Dickins and Lane-Poole, p. 260.

11 Chaiklin, translator, C.T. Assendelft de Coningh, *A Pioneer in Yokohama*, Simmons is mentioned in this period manuscript as a "true apostle of charity who roamed around the slums of the Japanese city..." pp. 114-5 a description that accords with his reputation for self-sacrifice and dedication and service to the poor and dispossessed.

12 Morse, *Japan Day by Day*, volume I, p. 336. See also Hammersmith, "Ohio's John A. Bingham in Meiji Japan", pp. 64-7. Morse lauds the "foresight and thoroughness" of the measures the Japanese government took to prevent the spread of the disease

13 *Ronsheim*, Roll II, item 1228, Stevens to Bingham, November 11, 1878.

14 Fuess, "Informal Imperialism and the 1879 *Hesperia* Incident", p. 113; Huffman, p. 142.

15 *FRUS*, John Bingham to William Evarts, p. 303-4, item 934, August 11, 1879, item 940-941, August 18, 1879; p. 313, item 980, October 7, 1879.

16 Bird, *Unbeaten Tracks in Japan*, p. 251.

17 Fuess, "Informal Imperialism", p. 107. Fuess refers to the *Yubin hochi shimbun* and *Tokyo nichi nichi shimbun* articles that make this argument.

18 Taliaferro, *All the Great Prizes*, p. 131.

19 Keene, p. 317.

20 Young, p. 545.

Chapter Fourteen

1 Benfey, *The Great Wave*, p. 52. Controversy over Agassiz' theory of polygenism and its contemporary relatives, scientific racism and creationism, continues into our own generation.
2 Huffman, p. 155.
3 Morse, *Japan Day by Day*, Volume I, p. 352.
4 Morse, Volume II, p. 200.
5 Brooks, *Fenollosa and His Circle*, p. 3.
6 Morse, Japan Day by Day, Volumes I and II.
7 Kijima and Thierry, "Translating 'natural selection' in Japanese", p. 30.
8 *Japan Mail*, February 15, 1879.
9 Secretary Evarts, Yale (Skull and Bones) and Harvard Law, a pedigree much more impressive than Bingham's years at Franklin College, shard Bingham's approach to Japan and their correspondence was consistently cordial.
10 Greene, *A New Englander in Japan*, p. 180. Greene also complained about a certain consular officer, clearly Van Buren. While he may have been critical of Bingham, to his more polished East Coat friends, Greene's low regard for Van Buren and his close connections with the missionary power center and the eastern educational elite on balance were helpful to Bingham.
11 Chamberlain, "In Memoriam, David Murray", from a collection of historical records of the State Street Presbyterian Church, Albany, New York, held in Allen County Public Library. Chamberlain quotes Bingham's dinner speech of 1875.
12 David Thompson's notebook.
13 *Ronsheim*, Roll II, item 1194, Lewis Lawton to John Bingham, April 1, 1878.
14 *Grant Papers*, volume 29, item 335, p. 301. Grant letter to Bingham, November 16, 1879.

Chapter Fifteen

1 *Ronsheim*, roll II, item 1118 and item 1129, December 1876, January 23, 1877.
2 *Ronsheim*, roll II, item 1200. May 22, 1878.
3 *Grant Papers*, Volume 30, pp. 149-51.
4 House, Edward, personal papers University of Virginia, J. R.

Young to House, December 1, 1879, December 19, 1879.
5 Huffman, p. 166.
6 *Grant Papers*, Volume 30, p. 151.
7 Inouye Kaoru's surname is sometimes written as Inoue. This latter is a more common romanization of the same surname in more recent times.
8 Paulin, "The Opening of Korea by Commodore Shufeldt", p. 480.
9 Paulin, p. 484.
10 Paulin, Charles Oscar, *Diplomatic Negotiations of American Naval Officers, 1778-1883*, p. 323. This source provides extensive portions of letters and other original documents.
11 *Grant Papers*, Volume 31, James Russell Young to Ulysses S. Grant, September 23, 1882, p. 444. It was common to spell Korea as Corea, a Romanization that still is used in Latin languages.
12 Cook, *Pioneer American Businessman in Korea*, pp. 20-22; Lepach, website manager, *Meiji Portraits*, 2017. This website in German, English and Japanese has extensive biographical information on hundreds of foreigners active in Japan during the Meiji era.
13 Beauregard, *Bingham of the Hills*, p. 173.
14 Conroy, p. 186.

Chapter Sixteen

1 Candice, *Destiny of the Republic*, p. 141. As noted earlier, the 1873 petition to Congress signed by 452 college and local educational officials from around the country had been circulated by the faculty of Williams College. See *Congressional Globe*, January 27, 1873, p. 891.
2 *Grant Papers*, Volume 30, Ulysses S. Grant to Chester A. Arthur, December 5, 1881, p. 307.
3 *Tokio Times*, May 8, 1880.
4 *Tokio Times*, various Spring 1880.
5 Huffman, p. 166.
6 Murphy, "Birdsey Grant Northrup", Kent, Connecticut Historical Society, February 2016, website article.
7 Kawasaki, "On the John Armor Bingham Papers", p. 39.
8 Jones, *Extraterritoriality in Japan*, p. 98-9. The Japan America Society of New York cooperated to make this study available.
9 Perez, *Japan Comes of Age*, p. 75.

10 Magliocca, p. 127.

11 Tsuda went on to found a school for women, now Tsuda University, in 1900. Tsuda University, in Tokyo, is among Japan's most prestigious schools.

12 Nimura, *Daughters of the Samurai*, p. 142.

13 Kuno, *Unexpected Destination*, pp. 103-4.

14 Kayaoglu, Turan, University of Washington, Seattle. Working paper for Comparative Graduate Student Retreat, San Diego, May 2004. Kayaoglu notes that extraterritoriality was abolished in the following years in the listed countries. Japan, 1899; Turkey, 1924; Thailand, 1925; Iran, 1928 and China, 1943.

Chapter Seventeen

1 Dennett, p. 580. Quoting Department of the Treasury Statistics published in 1904.

2 Murphy, p. 36.

3 Murphy, p. 148.

4 *Japan Mail*, September 24, 1881.

5 *Japan Mail*, October 1, 1881.

6 *Japan Mail*, October 15, 1881.

7 Meiji Portraits Listed alphabetically in the W's.

8 *Japan Mail*, November 19, 1881.

9 Chernow, *Titan: The Life of John D. Rockefeller, Sr.*, p. 211.

10 Free, pp. 42-53.

11 Lydia Hamilton Smith, who had an African-American grandparent, was hostess for Stevens' household and considered as his "companion". Stevens' strong anti-slavery leanings earned him particular opprobrium by Lost Cause proponents. Quoted in Wineapple, *Ecstatic Nation*, p. 427, the racist D.W. Griffiths' film, *Birth of a Nation*, refers to Stevens as "…a scowling cripple of lascivious tastes and pernicious intent."

12 Free, pp. 120-123. In later life, as further evidence of his political interest, Porter was elected to Congress in 1902. Biographical Directory of the United States Congress http://bioguide.congress.gov/scripts/biodisplay.pl?index=P000441

13 *FRUS*, Volume 1881-2, item 422, John Bingham to Secretary Evarts, February 9, 1881.

14 Free, p. 147. Ericson, "Importing Locomotives in Meiji Japan", p. 137. By the late 1890s, total American exports of locomotives exceeded those from British makers. The reasons for American

success included price, less delay in delivery, and stationing representatives in Japan rather than working mostly through trading companies. But the dogged support of the American Legation, first under Bingham, and then his successors contributed to this success story. *History of Baldwin Locomotive Works*, p. 81. Baldwin sold its first locomotives to Japan in June, 1887, for use in the Mie Kie coal mines.

Chapter Eighteen

1 Beauregard, *Bingham of the Hills*, p. 171.
2 Jones, *Extraterritoriality in Japan*, p. 128.
3 California did not ratify the 14th amendment until 1959.
4 *FRUS*, Volume 1883, p. 602, item 1595, Frelinghuysen letter to Bingham, March 21, 1883.
5 *FRUS*, Volume 1883, p. 604, item 1671, Bingham to Frelinghuysen, April 30, 1883.
6 *Ronsheim*, roll III, item 1482, 1484, Robert R. Hitt to John Bingham, January 15, 1885.
7 *Ronsheim*, roll III, item 1467, Bingham to Frelinghuysen, date unclear, September or October 1884.
8 *Ronsheim*, roll III, item 1484, Robert R. Hitt to John Bingham, January 15, 1885
9 *FRUS*, Volume 1885-1886, p. 554, item 1975, Bingham to Frelinghuysen, December 22, 1884.
10 *FRUS*, Volume 1885-1886, p. 554, item 1975, Bingham to Frelinghuysen, December 22, 1884.
11 *Ronsheim*, roll III, item 1688, John Swift to John Bingham, March 20, 1890.
12 Trani, *The Treaty of Portsmouth*, p. 73.
13 For the talks, Russian and Japanese negotiators stayed in Portsmouth, New Hampshire, and ferried across the Piscataqua River for the meetings which were held in the Portsmouth Naval Shipyard, in Kittery, Maine. For facilitating the talks, President Theodore Roosevelt was awarded the Nobel Peace Prize and for Foreign Minister Komora Jutaro, the favorable outcome of the negotiations was a major accomplishment.
14 Takahira, Koguro, *North American Review*, Volume 188, No. 632, July, 1908, pp. 13-14. This piece is an obituary for D. Stevens by the Japanese Minister to the United States.
15 Hoshi, *Japan and America*, pp. 13-15.

16 Takahira Koguro, p. 19.

17 Jones, *Live Machines*, p. 103; Shidehara, *Fifty Years of Diplomacy*

18 McHale, Jonathan R., *A History of the American Ambassador's Residence in Tokyo*, U.S. Embassy brochure, published in 1995.

19 Nippon Broadcasting (NHK), "The Constitution at Seventy" Broadcast April 30, 2017. (Japanese)

20 *Ronsheim*, roll IV, item 1728, Edwin Dun to John Bingham, August 6, 1891.

21 *Ronsheim*, roll II, item 1415, February 2, 1883.

22 Van Buren, *Labor in Japan.*

23 *Ronsheim*, roll II, item 1401, October 2, 1882.

24 *Japan Mail*, May 17, 1884.

25 *Japan Mail*, September 20, 1882.

26 *Japan Mail*, September 30, 1882.

27 *Ronsheim* roll V, John Bingham to Frazier (senior), February 5, 1883. This letter is among others that were kept separately and not in chronological order in the documents left behind when Bingham died. Many of the documents in this part of the collection are more personal and revealing than many of the more business-like documents in the rest of the collection.

28 *Congressional Record*, December 27, 1882, p. 663.

29 Cunningham, "Recreant to His Trust". This is an excellent review of the career of James Wasson, well-researched, well-written.

30 Whitney, *Diary*, Glimpses of the Binghams in various venues are occasionally available in these diaries.

31 *Clara's Diary*, see bibliography.

32 Whitney, *Clara's Diary*, p. 344.

33 Hommes, *Verbeck of Japan*, p. 124.

34 *Japan Mail*, August 19, 1884. In this article, Bingham friend and missionary George William Knox gives a guardedly optimistic assessment of the prospects for growth of Protestant Christianity in Japan.

35 *Ronsheim*, roll III, item 1484, Frelinghuysen to Bingham, March 26, 1885.

Conclusion

1 *Japan Weekly Mail*, July 18, 1885.

2 Hammersmith, *Spoilsmen*, p. 126. Hammersmith notes that

Bingham and the English language press "…feuded for the better part of a decade."

3 Foster, *American Diplomacy in the Orient*, p. 357.

4 Takahira, Kogoro, *The North American Review*, Vol. 188, No. 632 (July 1908), p.

5 *Ronshiem*, Roll III, item 1579.

6 Shotwell, *Driftwood*, p. 231.

7 Magliocca, *American Founding Son*.

8 The work of Richard Aynes, listed in the bibliography, is particularly important for the detailed information and depth of analysis of Bingham's life and career.

9 On July 12, 2018, the National Constitution Center in Philadelphia, partnered with the Thurgood Marshall Institute at the NAACP Legal Defense and Education Fund held a day long symposium on the 14th amendment. Bingham's role figured prominently in the speakers' presentations.

10 https://mansfieldfdn.org/ The website of the Maureen and Mike Mansfield Foundation has a page entitled "In his own voice" in which Ambassador Mansfield explains his use of the "bar none" expression.

BIBLIOGRAPHY

Abe, Ijuo. "Muscular Christianity in Japan: The Growth of a Hybrid." In *Muscular Christianity and the Colonial and Post-Colonial World.* John J. MacAloon, ed. 714-738. New York: Rutledge, 2008.

Adams, Henry. *The Education of Henry Adams.* New York: Oxford University Press, 1999.

Allardice, Bruce. *More Generals in Grey.* Baton Rouge: Louisiana, Louisiana University Press, 1995.

Althouse, Sue. "A Missionary Calling: A Day Causing Us to Pray Much." Website of Presbyterian Historical Society, March 4, 2016. https://www.history.pcusa.org/blog/2016/03/missionary-calling-day-causing-us-pray-much

Amar, Akhil Reed, "Did the 14th Amendment Incorporate the Bill of Rights Against the States?" (1996). *Faculty Scholarship Series.* Paper 996.

Amar, Akhil Reed. *The Bill of Rights, Creation and Reconstruction.* New Haven: Yale University Press, 1998.

Ambler, Charles. *Sectionalism in Virginia.* Chicago: University of Chicago Press,1910.

Auslin, Michael. *Negotiating with Imperialism: the Unequal Treaties and the Culture of Japanese Diplomacy.* Cambridge and London: Harvard University Press, 2004.

Aynes, Richard. "The Antislavery and Abolitionist Background of John A. Bingham." *Catholic University Law Review* 37, No. 4 (Summer, 1988): 881-933.

Aynes, Richard. "The Continuing Importance of John Bingham and the 14th Amendment." *Akron Law Review* 36, no. 4 (2003): 589-615.

Aynes, Richard. "Charles Fairman, Felix Frankfurter, and the 14th Amendment." *Chicago Kent Law Review* 70, No. 3 (1995): part II, 1197-1273.

Aynes, Richard. "John Bingham" in *The Yale Biographical Dictionary of American Law,* Newman, Roger, ed., New Haven, Connecticut: Yale University Press, 2009.

Aynes, Richard. "On Misreading John Bingham." *Yale Law Journal* 103, No. 1, (October 1993): 57-104.

Aynes, Richard. "Unintended Consequences of the 14th Amendment and What They Tell Us About Its Interpretation." *Akron Law Review* 39, No. 2 (2006): 289-321.

Baker, John. "Local History, Scotch-Irish Establish themselves in a New Land." *Times-Reporter*, New Philadelphia, Ohio (October 7, 2013).

Barr, Pat. *The Deer Cry Pavilion*. New York: Macmillian and Co,, Ltd, 1968.

Beasley, W. G. *The Meiji Restoration*. Stanford: Stanford University Press, 1972.

Beauregard, Erving E. "President Lincoln and Congressman Bingham." *Upper Ohio Valley Historical Review* (1990/1991): 18-35.

Beauregard, Erving E. *Bingham of the Hills*. New York: Peter Lang Publishing, 1989.

Beauregard, Erving E. *Reverend John Walker*. New York: Peter Lang Publishing, 1990.

Beauregard, Erving E. "Ohio's Fist Black College Graduate." *Queen City Heritage* 45 (1987): 19-26.

Beauregard, Erving E. "Samuel MaGill Bryan." *Journal of Asian History* 26, No. 1(1992): 31-41.

Benfey, Christopher, *The Great Wave: Gilded Age Misfits, Japan's Eccentrics, and the Opening of Old Japan*. New York: Random House, 2003.

Bible, King James Version. Varied opinions on origins and dates.

Bingham, John. *Harrisonian: Journal of the Harrison County, Ohio, Historical Society*, Number 3, (1990). In this edition, the Harrison County Historical Society reprinted the text of a reminiscence Bingham had written about his interactions with President Lincoln.

Bingham, John. *The Sectional Party*. Washington, D.C.: pamphlet published by Republican Executive Congressional Committee, 1860. https://archive.org/details/presidentsmessag00bing

Biographical Cyclopedia and Portrait Gallery of the State of Ohio. Cincinnati, Ohio: Western Biographical Publishing Company, 1884. http://ur0.work/IrYg

Birchford, Maynard. *The Life of John A. Bingham*. Madison, Wisconsin, unpublished Master's Thesis, University of Wisconsin, Department of History, 1951.

Bird, Isabella. *Unbeaten Tracks in Japan*. Mineola, New York: Dover Publishing, 2005. This edition is an unabridged republication of the work first published by John Murray, London, 1911.

Blight, David W. *Race and Reunion*. Cambridge, Massachusetts: Harvard University Press, 2001.

Blight, David W. "Slavery Did Not Die Honestly." *Atlantic* (October 21, 2015).https://www.theatlantic.com/politics/archive/2015/04/the-civil-war-isnt-over/389847/

Brooks, Van Wyck. *Fenollosa and His Circle*. New York: E.P. Dutton, 1962.

Burks, Ardath. "Coercion in Japan: A Historical Footnote." *The Journal of the Rutgers University Library* XV, No. 2 (June, 1952).

Bush, Lewis. *77 Samurai*. Tokyo, Palo Alto: Kodansha, 1968. Based on earlier book by Itsuro Hattori

Calhoun, Charles W. *From Bloody Shirt to Full Dinner Pail*. New York: Hill and Wang, 2010.

Calhoun, Charles. *The Presidency of Ulysses S. Grant*. Lawrence, Kansas: University of Kansas Press, 2017.

Campbell, Edwina. *Citizen of a Wider Commonwealth: Ulysses S. Grant's Presidential Diplomacy*. Carbondale, Illinois: Southern Illinois University Press, 2016.

Chaiklin, Martha. *A Pioneer in Yokohama: A Dutchman's Adventures in the New Treaty Port*. Indianapolis, Indiana: Hackett Publishing Company, 2012.

Chaiklin, Martha. "Monopolists to Middlemen: Dutch Liberalism in the Opening of Japan." *Journal of World History* 21, No. 2 (June, 2010).

Chamberlain, William Isaac. *In Memoriam: Dr. David Murray: Ph.D., LL.D., Superintendent of Educational Affairs in the Empire of Japan*. From documents in the collection of the State Street Presbyterian Church, Albany, New York, held in the Allen County Library, Albany, New York.

Chang, Richard. "General Grant's 1879 Visit to Japan." *Monumenta Nipponica* 24, No. 4 (1969), 3.

Checkland, Olive. *Britain's Encounter with Meiji Japan, 1868-1912*. London: Palgrave Macmillan, 1989.

Chernow, Ron. *Grant*. New York: Penguin Press, 2017.

Chernow, Ron. *Titan: John D. Rockefeller, Sr.* New York: Random House, 1998.

Choe, Ching Young. *The Rule of the Taewongun, 1864-1873, Restoration in Yi Korea.* Cambridge, Massachusetts: Harvard University Monograph Series 45, 1972.

Colcutt Martin, Kato, Mikio and Toby, Ronald. *Japan and its Worlds, Marius B. Jansen and the Internationalization of Japanese Studies.* Tokyo: I-House Press, 2007. Includes Colcutt. "Education for a New Japan: Kume Kunitake's Observations on Education in 1872 America" 187-208.

Conant, Ellen. *Challenging the Past and Present: The Metamorphosis of Nineteenth-Century Japanese Art.* Honolulu: University of Hawaii Press, 2006.

Conroy, Hilary, *The Japanese Seizure of Korea.* Philadelphia: University of Pennsylvania Press, 1960.

Cook, Harold F. *Pioneer American Businessman in Korea: The Life and Times of Walter Davis Townsend.* Seoul: Royal Asiatic Society, 1981.

Copeland, Rebecca. "All Other Loves Excelling: Mary Kidder and Wakamatsu Shizuko and Modern Marriage in Meiji Japan." Hyaeweol Choi and Margaret Jolly, eds., *Divine Domesticities: Christian Paradoxes in Asia and the Pacific.* Canberra, Australia: Australian University Press, 2014.

Cunningham, Roger D. "Recreant to His Trust: The Disappointing Career of Major James R. Wasson." *The Professional Bulletin of Army History.* Winter/Spring 2004.

Curtis, Michael Kent. "John A. Bingham and the Story of American Liberty: the Lost Cause Meets the Lost Clause." *Akron Law Review* 36, No. 4 (2003: 617-669.

Daniels, Gordon. *Sir Harry Parkes: British Representative in Japan 1865-83.* Surrey, Richmond: Imprint of Curazon Press by Japan Library, 1996.

Dare, Philip N. *John A. Bingham and Treaty Revision with Japan: 1873-1885."* unpublished PhD dissertation, University of Kentucky. Lexington, Kentucky: 1975.

Dennett, Tyler. *Americans in East Asia: A Critical Study of the Policy of the United States with Reference to China, Japan and Korea.* New York, Boston, Chicago: Macmillan Company, 1922.

Dickins, F.V. *The Life of Sir Harry Parkes: Minister Plenipotentiary to Japan.* Volume II. London: Macmillan and Company, 1894.

Dickins, Frederick Victor and Lane-Poole, Stanley. *The Life of Sir Harry Parkes.* Two volumes in five volume series of *Collected Works of F.V, Dickens.* London and New York: Macmillan and Company, 1894.

Documenting the American South. Website with reference of Bingham Mercer County colleague, lawyer John J. Pearson and feed slave John Quincy Adams. http://docsouth.unc.edu/neh/adams/adams.html

Donnelly, Thomas, *Constitution Daily.* Website of National Constitution Center, Philadelphia,
July 9, 2018. https://constitutioncenter.org/interactive-constitution/podcast/happy-150th-birthday-14th-amendment#

Dower, John W. "Yokohama Boomtown." *Visualizing Cultures.* Cambridge, Massachusetts, MIT website, online article posted 2015. https://ocw.mit.edu/ans7870/21f/21f.027/yokohama/index.html

Downs, Gregory. *After Appomattox, Military Occupation and the Ends of War.* Cambridge, Massachusetts: Harvard University Press, 2015.

Duke, Benjamin C. *The History of Modern Japanese Education.* New Brunswick, New Jersey: Rutgers University Press, 2009.

Dun, Edwin. *Reminiscences of Nearly Half a Century in Japan.* Autobiography in the archives of the U.S. Department of Agriculture, National Agricultural Library. Japanese version produced by Nishide and Kawabata, 1992.

Eckert, Carter. *Offspring of Empire: The Koch'ang Kims and the Colonial Origins of Korean Capitalism, 1876-1945.* Seattle: University of Washington Press, 1991.

Epps, Garrett. *Democracy Reborn: The 14th amendment and the Fight for Equal rights in Post-Civil War America.* New York: Henry Holt, 2006.

Ericson, Steven J. "Importing Locomotives in Meiji Japan: International Business and Technology Transfer in the Railroad Industry" *Osiris University of Chicago Press*, Volume 13 (1998: 129-53.

Ericson, Steven J. *The Sound of the Whistle: Railroads and the State in Meiji Japan.* Cambridge: Harvard University Press, 1996.

Eskildsen, Robert. "Of Civilization and Savages: The Memetic Imperialism of Japan's 1874 Expedition to Taiwan." *The American Historical*

Review 107, No. 2, (April 2002): 388-418.

Eskildsen, Robert. "Whither East Asia? Reflections on Japan's Colonial Experience in Taiwan" *Asia-Pacific Journal* volume 3, issue 11, (November 24, 2005).

Fenollosa, Ernest. *East and West*. New York and Boston: Thomas Y. Crowell and Company, 1893. Google reprint, Harvard University Bookstore.

Foner, Eric. *Reconstruction: America's Unfinished Revolution, 1863-77*. New York: Harper and Row, 1988.

Foster, John Watson. *Diplomatic Memoirs*. London: Constable, 1910.

Franklin College Register: Biographical and Historical. Wheeling, West Virginia: West Virginia Printing Company, 1908. https://catalog. hathitrust.org/Record/100114321

Fraser, Andrew. "The Osaka Conference of 1875." *The Journal of Asian Studies* 26, No. 44 (August 1967): 589-610.

Frazer Persifor. "In Memory of Edward Yorke McCauley, U.S.N." *Proceedings of the American Philosophical Society* 34, No. 149 (1895): 364-380. https://www.biodiversitylibrary.org/part/211951#/ summary

Free, Dan. *Early Japanese Railways, 1853-1914*. Tokyo, Rutland, Vermont: Tuttle Publishing, 2008.

Fuess, Harald. "Informal Imperialism and the 1879 *Hesperia* Incident: Containing Cholera and Challenging Extraterritoriality." *Japan Review* 27 (2014): 103-140.

Fujita, Fumiko. *American Pioneers and the Japanese Frontier*. Westport, Connecticut, London: Greenwood Press, 1994.

Goodman, Paul. *Abolitionism and the Origins of Racial Equality*. Berkeley, California: University of California Press, 1998.

Gordon, Andrew. *A Modern History of Japan: From Tokugawa Times to the Present*. New York and Oxford: Oxford University Press, 2003.

Grant, Ulysses S. letter in archives of Harrison County Historical Society. Grant to Bingham, dated November 16, 1879, thanking Bingham for his help while in Japan. See also *Ronsheim* and Morgan Library collections.

Green, Evarts Boutell. *A New Englander in Japan: Daniel Crosby Greene*. New York: Houghton Mifflin, 1927.

Grew, Joseph, *Ten Years in Japan*. New York: Simon and Schuster, *1944*.

Griffis, William Elliot. A Maker of the New Orient: Samuel Robbins Brown, Pioneer Educator in China, America and Japan. New York, Chicago, Toronto: Fleming H. Revell Co., 1914.

Griffis, William Elliot. *Address at Kirkpatrick Chapel, Rutgers College delivered June 16, 1885*. Published for Rutgers College Alumni Association by Wee, Parsons and Company, printers, 1886.

Griffs, William Elliot. *Hepburn of Japan and His Wife and Helpmates: A Life of Toil for Christ*. Philadelphia: Westminster Press, 1913. Reprint Forgotten Books, 2012.

Griffs, William Elliot. *Verbeck of Japan, A Citizen of No Country*. New York, Chicago, Toronto: Fleming H. Revell Co., 1900. Reprint Forgotten Books 2012.

Guthrie-Shimizu, Sayuri. *Transpacific Field of Dreams, How Baseball Linked the United States in Peace and War*. Chapel Hill, North Carolina: University of North Carolina Press, 2012.

Hagin, Fred. *The Cross in Japan*. New York, Chicago, Toronto: Fleming H. Revell Co, 1914.

Hall, Ivan Parker. *Mori Arinori*. Cambridge, Massachusetts: Harvard University Press, 1973.

Hammersmith, Jack. "Ohio's John A. Bingham in Meiji Japan: The Politician as Diplomat," *Ohio History* 126; 1 (Spring 2019), pp. 58-71.

Hammersmith, Jack L. *Spoilsmen in a "Flowery Fairyland."* Kent, Ohio: Kent State University Press, 1998.

Hanna, Charles Augustus. *Historical Collections of Harrison County in the State of Ohio*. Privately published by resident of Cadiz, Ohio, 1900. https://archive.org/details/oh-harrison-1900-hanna

Hardman, Keith J. *Charles Grandison Finney: Revivalist and Reformer*. Grand Rapids, Michigan: Baker Book House, 1987.

Hemphill, Robert. *A Church for All Seasons: Tokyo Union Church 1872-1980*. Published by Tokyo Union Church on the occasion of the church's centennial celebration 1972. Updated edition 1980.

Henry Willard Denison, Son of Lancaster, Counsel to the Japanese Foreign

Ministry, website of Japan America Society of New Hampshire, March 17, 2016. http://www.portsmouthpeacetreaty.com/lancaster. cfm

Hialt, Anna. "This History of Cremation in Japan," *JSTOR Daily*, (September 9, 2015). https://daily.jstor.org/history-japan-cremation/

History of Mercer County, Chicago: Brown, Runk & Co., 1888, https:// archive.org/details/historyofmercerc00unse

History of Tuscarawas County. Chicago: Warner, Beers and Company, 1884. https://books.google.com/books/about/The_History_of_ Tuscarawas_County_Ohio.html?id=5DguAAAAYAAJ

History of the Mercer County Courthouse. Website of Mercer County, Pennsylvania. https://www.mcc.co.mercer.pa.us/history/courthouse. htm

Hitchcock, Mary E. *Two Women in the Klondike*. Fairbanks, Alaska: University of Alaska Press, 2005.

Hommes, James Mitchell. *Verbeck of Japan: Guido Verbeck as Pioneer Missionary, Oyatoi Gaikokujin and "Foreign Hero"*. Unpublished PhD dissertation, University of Pittsburgh. Pittsburgh, Pennsylvania: 2014.

Honjo, Yuki Allyson. *Japan's Early Experience of Contract Management in the Treaty Ports*. New York: Routledge, 2013.

House, Edward. *The Japanese Expedition to Formosa*. Paper published by author in Tokyo, 1875.

Howland, Douglas. Society Reified: "Herbert Spencer and Political Theory in Early Meiji Japan." *Comparative Studies in Society and History* 42, No. 1 (January 2000): 67-86.

Howland, Douglas. *Translating the West: Language and Political Reason in Nineteenth Century Japan*. Honolulu: University of Hawaii Press, 2002.

Huffman, James A. *A Yankee in Meiji Japan*. Lanham, Maryland: Rowman and Littlefield Publishers, Inc., 2003.

Hughes, Thomas. *Tom Brown's School Days*. London: Macmillan, 1857. Google reprint.

Hunt, William E. *Historical Collections of Coshocton County, Ohio*. Cincinnati, Ohio: R. Clarke & Co., printers, 1876. https://archive.

org/details/historicalcollec00hunt

International Conference on Education Held at Philadelphia, July 17 and 18. Washington, D.C.: Department of the Interior, Bureau of Education, Government Printing Office, 1877. Reprint by Abe Books.

Ion, Hamish. *American Missionaries, Christian Oyatoi and Japan 1859-73*. Vancouver, British Columbia: UBC Press, 2009.

Iryie, Kira. *Japan and the Wider World from the Nineteenth Century to the Present*. London and New York: Longman, 1997.

Iwata Masakazu. *Okubo Toshimichi: The Bismark of Japan*. Berkeley, University of California Press, 1964.

Jansen, Marius. *The Making of Modern Japan*. Cambridge, Massachusetts: The Belknap Press of Harvard University Press, 2000.

Jones, F.C. *Extraterritoriality in Japan and the Diplomatic Relations Resulting in Its Abolition*. New York: AMS Press, 1931, (reprint made available in 1970 by Japan Society of New York)

Jones, H. J. *Live Machines: Hired Foreigners and Meiji Japan*. Vancouver, British Columbia: UBC Press, 1980.

Kahan, Paul. *The Presidency of Ulysses S. Grant*. Yardley, Pennsylvania: Westholme, 2018.

Karp, Matthew. *This Vast Southern Empire: Slaveholders at the Helm of American Foreign Policy*. Cambridge, Massachusetts: Harvard University Press, 2016.

Kayaoglu, Turan. University of Washington, Seattle. Working paper Comparative Graduate Student Retreat, San Diego, May 2004.

Kawasaki Seiro. "On the John Armor Bingham Papers." *Kasai University Journal 2*, (1998) 35-40.

Kawasaki Seiro. "Origins of the Stone Tablets on the St. Luke's Hospital Grounds." *Kasai University Journal 2* (1998): 19-33.

Kawasaki Seiro. *Tsukiji Foreign Residential Quarter*. Tokyo: Yusho Do, 2011. (Japanese)

Keene, Donald. *Emperor of Japan: Meiji and His World, 1852-1912*. New York: Columbia University Press, 2002.

Kijjima Taizo and Hoquet Thierry. "Translating 'Natural Selection'

into Japanese." *Binomia* (International Journal of Biological
Nomenclature and Terminology) 6, Magnolia Press (2013): 26-48.

Kingdom of Hawaii – Constitution of 1840 Website of the Native
Hawaiian Bar Association. http://www.alohaquest.com/archive/
constitution_1840.htm

Knox, George William. *The Development of Religion in Japan.* New York:
Knickerbocker Press, G.P. Putnam's Sons, 1907.

Kogura Takahira. "Durham White Stevens". *The North American Review*
159, Issue 454, No. 632 (July 1908), 12-20.

Komura Jutaro. *Meiji's Hidden Diplomatic History.* Tokyo: Hara Shobo,
1977. (Japanese)

Kume Kunitake, compiled and edited by Chushichi Tsuzuki and R. Jules
Young. *Japan Rising: The Iwakura Embassy to the USA and Europe
1871-1873.* London: Cambridge University Press, 2009.

Kuno, Akiko. *(Kristen McIvor translator) Unexpected Destination, the
Poignant Story of Japan's First Vassar Graduate.* Tokyo, London, New
York: Kodansha, International, 1993.

Kurian Thomas and Lamport, Mark, eds. *Encyclopedia of Christianity in the
United States.* Lanham, Maryland: Rowman and Littlefield, 2016.

LaFeber, Walter. *The Clash: U.S. – Japan Relations Throughout History.* New
York: W. W. Norton & Co., 1997.

LeGendre, Charles William. *Progressive Japan.* New York: C. Levy, 1878.

Lepach, Bernd. *Meiji Portraits.* http://www.meiji-portraits.de/meiji_
portraits_s.html

Lexington, Kentucky: University of Kentucky Press, 1969.

Leyburn, James G. *The Scotch Irish: A Social History.* Chapel Hill, North
Carolina: University of North Carolina Press, 1962.

Li, Victor. "The 14th: A Civil War Amendment Has Become a Mini-
Constitution for Modern Times." *Journal of the American Bar
Association* (May 2017), cover story. http://www.abajournal.com/
magazine/article/14th_amendment_constitution_important_today

Light Locomotives, H. K. Porter and Co., Pittsburgh, Pennsylvania, 1889.
Catalogue.

Lowell, Percival. *Soul of the Far East.* Cambridge, Massachusetts:

Houghton, Mifflin and Company, the Riverside Press, 1888.

Magliocca, Gerard. *American Founding Son: John Bingham and the Invention of the 14th Amendment*. New York: New York University Press, 2013.

Maki, John. *A Yankee in Hokkaido: the Life of William Smith Clark*. Lanham, Maryland: Rowman and Littlefield, 2002.

Marvel, William. *Lincoln's Autocrat: the Life of Edwin Stanton*. Chapel Hill, North Caroline: University of North Carolina Press, 2015.

Maxfield, Charles A. "The Legacy of Jeremiah Evarts," *International Bulletin of Missionary Research*, New Haven, Connecticut: Overseas Mission Studies Center, October 1998.

Mayo, Marlene J. "A Catechism of Western Diplomacy: The Japanese and Hamilton Fish, 1872." *Journal of Asian Studies* 26, No. 3 (May 1967): 389-410.

Mayo, Marlene J. "The Korean Crisis of 1873 and Early Meiji Foreign Policy." *Journal of Asian Studies* 31, No. 4, (August 1972): 793-819.

McCollough, Steven. "Avoiding War: The Foreign Policy of Ulysses S. Grant and Hamilton Fish," in *A Companion to the Reconstruction Presidents, 1865-1881*, Franz, Edward O., ed. Chichester, West Sussex, UK, 2004.

McCune, George. "The Exchange of Envoys Between Korea and Japan in the Tokugawa Period." *Far Eastern Quarterly* 5:3 (May 1946).

McGavran, S.B., Dr. *A Brief History of Harrison County, Ohio*. Cadiz, Ohio: published by Harrison Tribune, May 1894.

McHale, Jonathan. *A History of the American Ambassador's Residence in Tokyo*. Tokyo, Japan, American Embassy, 1995.

Millard, Candice. *Destiny of the Republic: A Tale of Madness, Medicine and the Murder of a President*. New York: Anchor Books a division of Random House, 2012.

Mizuno Asao. *Tsukiji Kyoruychi (Tsukiji Residential District) . Volume 4* Tokyo: Tsukiji Residential District Research Society, 2015. (Japanese)

Mizuno, Norihito. "Qing China's Reaction to the 1874 Japanese Expedition to the Taiwanese Aboriginal Territories." *Sino-Japanese Studies* 16, article 8, (2009).

Moore, George. "Samurai Conversion: The Case of Kumamoto." *Asian Studies* 4, No. 1, Manila (April 1966): 40-48.

Mori Arinori. *Life and Resources in America*. Edited and annotated by John E. Van Sant. Lanham, Maryland: Lexington Books, 2004.

Morley, James. *Japan's Foreign Policy,1868-1941*. New York: Columbia University Press, 1974.

Morrison, Joseph M. "Argument of Joseph M. Morrison before the sub-committee of the Committee on foreign affairs of the House of representatives on the Japanese indemnity fund." Washington D.C.: Library of Congress, 1878. https://archive.org/details/argumentofjoseph00morr

Morse, Edward. *Japan Day by Day, 1877, 1878-9, 1882-3 Vol I and II.* Boston: Houghton Mifflin, 1917. Reprint by Harvard Bookstore.

Murphy, Kevin C. *The American Merchant Experience in Nineteenth Century Japan*. London and New York: RoutledgeCurzon, Taylor & Francis Group, 2003.

Murphy, Wendy. "Birdsey Grant Northrup, Tree Hugger Extraordinaire", Kent, Connecticut Historical Society Newsletter, February 2016. http://kenthistoricalsociety.org/birdsey-grant-northrop-tree-hugger-extraordinaire/

Nagai Michio. "Herbert Spencer in Early Meiji Japan." *The Far Eastern Quarterly* 42, No. 1 (January 2000), 67-86.

Nakagawa Yoshiaki. "B.C. Northrup Reconsidered." *Historical Society of English Studies in Japan*. (1982): 113-123. (Japanese)

Nakajima, Koji. " Diplomacy and missionaries in Modern Japan." Yoshikawa Kobunkan. (2012) (Japanese)

Neuman, William L. *America Encounters Japan from Perry to MacArthur*. Johns Hopkins Press: Baltimore, 1963.

Nevins, Allan. *Hamilton Fish: The Inner History of the Grant Administration*. New York: Dodd, Mead and Company, 1937.

Nimura, Janice P. *Daughters of the Samurai: A Journey from East to West and Back*. New York: W.W. Norton and Company, 2015.

Nish, Ian, *The Iwakura Mission to American and Europe: A New Assessment*. Note article on Italy portion of the trip by Silvana de Maio, p. 100. Abingdon, UK: Routledge, 2008.

Nolan, Dick. *Benjamin Franklin Butler.* Novato, CA: Presidio Press, 1991.

Nootbar, Julie Joy. "Charles Longfellow's Twenty Months in Japan." *Oita College of Art and Culture Journal* 52 (2015): 107-121.

Noteheller, F.G. *American Samurai Captain: L.L. Janes and Japan.* Princeton, New Jersey: Princeton University Press, 1985.

Noteheller, F.G. *Japan Through American Eyes: The Journal of Francis Hall 1859-1866.* Boulder, Colorado: Westview Press, 2001. Original journal in possession of Cleveland Public Library.

Ohio Law Bulletin 8. Norwalk, Ohio: (1903) 36.

Okabu Kazuoki, ed. *Opening of the Yokohama Port and Protestant Missionaries (Yokohama Kaikou to Senkyoshi tachi).* Yokohama: Yokohama Protestant Historical Society, Yulindo (Yulin Press), 1978. (Japanese)

Okamoto Kikuko. "A Cultural History of Planting Memorial Trees in Modern Japan: With a Focus on General Grant in 1979". *Journal of the Graduate University of Advanced Studies, School of Cultural and Social Studies Vol. 9* (2013) 81-97. Japanese and English versions available.

Okazaki, Hisahiko. *A Century of Japanese Diplomacy.* Tokyo: Echo, Inc., 2002.

Otis, Gary. *A History of Christianity in Japan.* New York, Chicago, Toronto: Fleming H. Revell, 1909.

Palais, James B. *Politics and Policy in Traditional Korea.* Cambridge, Massachusetts: Harvard University Press, 1975.

Paulin, Charles Oscar. *Diplomatic Negotiations of American Naval Officers, 1778-1883.* Baltimore, Maryland: Johns Hopkins Press, 1912.

Paulin, Charles Oscar. "The Opening of Korea by Commodore Shufeldt." *Political Science Quarterly* 25, No. 3 (September 1910): 470-499.

Pendleton, Scott. "William H. Lucas: An Unusually Useful Life." Blog entry for Harrison _County Historical Society, dated April 3 2010.

Perez, Louis G. *Japan Comes of Age: Mutsu Munemitsu and the Revision of the Unequal Treaties.* Cranberry, New Jersey: Associated University Presses, Inc., 1999.

Perry, John Curtis. *Facing West: Americans and the Opening of the Pacific.* Westport, Connecticut: Praeger, 1994.

Perry, Matthew C. "A Paper by Commodore M.C. Perry, U.S.N., Read Before the American Geographical and Statistical Society." New York: D. Appleton and Company, 1856. Reprinted from original by Abe Books.

Pletcher, David. *The Diplomacy of Involvement: American Economic Expansion Across the Pacific*. Columbia, Missouri: University of Missouri Press, 2002.

Pumpelly, Raphael. *Travels and Adventures of Raphael Pumpelly*. New York: Henry Holt and Company, 1920.

Pyle, Kenneth B. *Japan Rising*. New York: Perseus Book Group, 2007.

Ravina, Mark. *To Stand with the Nations of the World*. New York: Oxford University Press, 2017.

Saito, Hiroshi. *Japan's Policies and Purposes*. Boston: Marshall Jones Company, 1935. This includes a full chapter on Henry Denison by a Japanese diplomat who served as Ambassador to the United States.

Satow, Ernest. *A Diplomat in Japan, Part II: The Diaries of Ernest Satow, 1870-1883*. Morrisville, North Carolina: Lulu Press Inc., 2009.

Schlictman, Klaus. *Japan in the World: Shidehara Kijuro, Pacifism and the Abolition of War*. London and New York: Lexington Books, 2009.

Seidensticker, Edward. *Tokyo: from Edo to Showa 1867-1989*. Tokyo, Rutledge, Vermont: Tuttle Publishing, 2010.

Seward, Olive Risley. *William H. Seward's Travels Around the World*. New York: D. Appleton, 1873.

Seward, William Henry. Speech to the Senate on the Admission of California and the Issue of Slavery. 1850 https://archive.org/details/williamhspeech00sewarich

Sewell, John S. "The Invincible Armada in Japan." *New England and Yale Review* 53 (1890): 201-212.

Shavit, David. *The United States in Asia: A Historical Dictionary*. New York: Greenwood Press, 1990.

Shewmaker, Kenneth E. "Forging the 'Great Chain': Daniel Webster and the Origins of American Policy Towards East Asia and the Pacific." *Proceedings of the American Philosophical Association* 129, No. 3 (September 1985): 225-259.

Shibusawa Eiichi. Craig, Teruko, translator. *The Autobiography of Shibusawa*

Eiichi: from Peasant to Entrepreneur. Tokyo: University of Tokyo Press, 1994.

Shidehara Kijuro, *Gaikyo Gojunen (Fifty Years of Diplomacy).* Tokyo: Chuokoron-Shinasa, Inc., 1987 reissued 2015. (Japanese)

Shotwell, Walter Gaton. *Driftwood.* New York: Longman, Green and Co., 1927.

Simmons, D.B. M.D. "Cholera Epidemics in Japan." Shanghai: Printed by the Statistical Department of the Inspectorate of Customs, 1879. http://u0u0.net/Is1R

Smethurst, Richard. *Takahashi Korekiyo: From Foot Soldier to Finance Minister.* Cambridge, Massachusetts and London: Harvard University Asia Center, Harvard East Asia Monograph Series, 2007.

Smith, George. *Ten Weeks in Japan.* London: Longman, Green and Longman, Roberts, 1861. https://archive.org/details/ tenweeksinjapan00smitgoog

Smith, Jean Edward. *Grant.* New York: Simon and Schuster, 2001.

Statement of the Proceedings of Citizens of Englewood, Bergen County, New Jersey, in Relation to the Suspension and Removal of Gen'l Thomas B. Van Buren, Officer of the Commissioner General, Universal Exposition at Vienna, 1873. https://www.bokus.com/ bok/9781332200047/a-statement-of-the-proceedings-of-citizens- of-englewood-bergen-county-new-jersey-in-relation-to-the- suspension-and-removal-of-genl-thomas-b-van-buren/

Stephenson, Samuel. "Charles William LeGendre, 26 August 1830- 1 September 1899." Entry in *Dictionary of American Biography,* Malone, D., ed. New York: Charles Scribner and Sons, 1960.

Stevens, Durham W. "China and Japan in Korea." *North American Review* 188, No. 632 (July 1908): 12-20.

Stewart, David O. *Impeached: The Trial of President Andrew Johnson and the Fight for Lincoln's Legacy.* New York: Simon and Schuster, 2009.

Strong, James and McClintock, John, *Cyclopedia of Biblical Theological and Ecclesiastical Literature.* New York: Harper and Brothers, 1890.

Sugiyama, Shinya. "The Impact of the Opening of the Ports on Domestic Japanese Industry: the Case of Silk and Cotton." *The Economic Studies Quarterly,* Volume 38 No. 4 (December 1987).

Sumner, Charles. *Charles Sumner His Complete Works Volume 18*. Boston: Lee and Shepard, 1880, 1882. Reprint edition by Lulu.

Swift, Donald C. "John Bingham and Reconstruction: The Dilemma of a Moderate." *Ohio History Journal* 1968. Published online by Ohio History Connection. http://resources.ohiohistory.org/ohj/browse/displaypages.php?display[]=0077&display[]=76&display[]=94

Taliafaro, John. *All the Great Prizes: The Life of John Hay from Lincoln to Roosevelt*. New York, Simon and Schuster, 2014.

The Harrisonian, Journal of the Harrison County Historical Association, Number 3, (1990).

Trani, Eugene P. *The Treaty of Portsmouth: An Adventure in American Diplomacy*.

Treat, Payson Jackson. *The Early Diplomatic Relations Between the United States and Japan, 1853-1865*. Baltimore: Johns Hopkins Press 1917.

Treat, Payson Jackson. "The Return of the Shimonoseki Indemnity." *The Journal of Race Development* 8, No. 1 (July, 1917), 1-12.

Umetani Noboru. "The Role of Foreign Employees in the Meiji Era in Japan." *Institute of Developing Economies Occasional Papers*, Series 9 (1971).

Van Buren, Thomas. *Labor in Japan*. Washington: Department of State, 1880.

Van Buren, Thomas. *Porcelain in Japan*. Washington: Department of State, 1881.

Van Sant, John E., Peter Mauch and Sugita Yoneyuki. *Historical Dictionary of United States – Japan Relations*. Lanham, Maryland: Rowman and Littlefield Publishers, Inc., 2007.

Virginia Military Institute Archives, https://www.vmi.edu/archives/digital-collections/

Wakimura Kohei. "Globalization Environment and Epidemic Disease: Cholera in 19th Century Asia." Monograph presented at XIV International History Conference, Session 46, Helsinki: 2006. http://www.helsinki.fi/iehc2006/papers2/Wakimura.pdf

Walsh Brothers, Mitsubishi Corporation website "Stories of Some Prominent Figures." https://www.mitsubishi.com/e/history/series/walsh/

Weber, Max. *The Protestant Ethic and the Spirit of Capitalism.* Translated by Talcott Parsons. New York: Charles Scribner and Sons, 1958. Original German edition 1904-5.

Weir, David. *American Orient: Imagining the East from the Colonial Era through the Twentieth Century.* Amherst and Boston: University of Massachusetts Press, 2011.

White, Ronald C. *American Ulysses: A Life of Ulysses S. Grant.* New York: Random House, 2016.

Whitman, Walt. *Leaves of Grass.* Mt. Vernon, New York: Peter Pauper Press, 1950.

Whitney Clara. Clara's Diary: *An American Girl in Meiji Japan.* William Steele and Tamiko Ichimata, editors. Tokyo: Kodansha International Ltd., 1979

Who Was William Sturgis Bigelow? Website of the Massachusetts Historical Society, 2001. https://www.masshist.org/objects/cabinet/may2002/bigelow.htm

Wiebe, Robert. *The Search for Order, 1877-1920.* New York: Hill and Wang, 1967.

Wiley, Richard T. "Lafayette in Western Pennsylvania." Paper read at the meeting of the Historical Society of Western Pennsylvania October 26, 1937. file:///Users/SamKidder/Downloads/2071-1918-1-PB%20(2).pdf

Willie, William P. *An Inside View of the Formation of the State of West Virginia.* Wheeling West Virginia: The News Publishing Company, 1901.

Wilson, Erasmus, editor. *Standard History of Pittsburgh, Pennsylvania.* Chicago: H.R. Cornell &Company, 1898.

Yates, Charles L. *Saigo Takamori: The Man Behind the Myth.* London and New York: Kegan Paul International, 1995.

Yokohama Protestant Historical Society, eds. *Missionaries and the Opening of Yokohama Port.* Yokohama: Yourin Publishing, 2015. (Japanese)

Young, John Russell. *Around the World with General Grant, Volume II.* New York: American News Company, 1879. Reprint Kessinger Legacy Reprints.

Zeitlow, Rebeca. "Congressional Enforcement of Civil rights and John Bingham's Theory of Citizenship." *Akron Law Review* 36, No. 4 (2003) 717-769.

"Submarine Cable History" Kokusai Cable Ship Co., Ltd. 2001. http://www.k-kcs.co.jp/english/cableHistory.html

"Thompson Papers Chronicle Family's Life in 19th Century Japan," website of the Presbyterian Historical Society, February 11, 2013. https://www.history.pcusa.org/blog/thompson-papers-chronicle-familys-life-19th-century-japan

Periodicals and Private Papers

Alumni Register of the University of Pennsylvania
Archives of the Ministry of Foreign Affairs (Japanese)
Atlantic Monthly 1876, 1881
Biographical Dictionary of the United States Congress 1774-2005. GPO
Cadiz Republican
Cadiz Sentinel
Congressional Globe
Congressional Record
Consular Reports on the Commerce, Manufacturers, Etc., of their Consular Districts
Daily Japan Herald, 1874-1875, 1877-1881
David Thompson Notebook, unpublished, Presbyterian Historical Society, Philadelphia.
Edward House Letters, Archives of the University of Virginia
Foreign Relations of the United States (FRUS)
Franklin College Register, Franklin College Board of Trustees
Harrisburg Patriot, 1888
Helena Herald, 1876
Japan Gazette, 1874-1886
Japan Times, 1878
Japan Weekly Mail, 1872-1886
JiJi Press (Japanese)

Letters of Edwin Dun, Obihiro University of Agriculture and Medicine
Mary Thompson Diary, unpublished, Presbyterian Historical Society,
    Philadelphia
Millard Fillmore Papers, Buffalo Historical Society
Miscellaneous Documents of the House of Representatives, 43rd Session, 1872-3
Missionary Correspondence, Board of Foreign Missions of the
    Presbyterian Church, microfilm, Presbyterian Historical Society,
    Philadelphia
Missionary Herald – publication of the American Board of Commissioners
    for Foreign Missions
Morgan Library Collection – John Armor Bingham Papers
New York Times, 1889, various
Oberlin College Archives
Official Register of the United States Officers and Employees GPO 1889.
Outline History of Japanese Education, Published by Japanese Ministry of
    Education, in English, 1876.
Papers of Eli T. Sheppard, Stanford University
Papers of Ulysses S. Grant – Mississippi State University
Papers Related to the Foreign Relations of the United States (PRFRUS)
Ronsheim Collection, Microfilm – Rutherford B. Hayes Library,
    Manuscripts Division
Rothesay Miller Letter, Missouri History Museum
San Francisco Call
Sharon (Pennsylvania) Herald 1888, 1966
The Christian Intelligencer
The Christian Work, 1901
Tokio Times, 1877-1880
Virginia Military Institute Archives
Washington and Jefferson College website

Perry was the first foreigner who opened the long-closed doors of Japan. If he was the introducer of his western civilization to Japan, Judge Bingham was its cultivator in the Japanese soil.

– From the speech of Komatsu Midori, Japanese representative to Bingham memorial service, Cadiz, Ohio, 1901. Photo from the Ohio History Connection

9 781950 381586